3 1994 01405 4545

4/10

SANTA ANA PUBLIC LIBRARY

ONE MORE THEORY ABOUT HAPPINESS

ALSO BY PAUL GUEST

The Resurrection of the Body and the Ruin of the World

Exit Interview

Notes for My Body Double

My Index of Slightly Horrifying Knowledge

ecco

An Imprint of HarperCollins*Publishers*

B GUEST, P. GUE
Guest, Paul
One more theory about
    happiness

CENTRAL $21.99
                  31994014054545

ONE

MORE

THEORY

ABOUT

HAPPINESS

A Memoir

PAUL GUEST

To protect the privacy of others, some names have been changed and identifying characteristics altered.

ONE MORE THEORY ABOUT HAPPINESS. Copyright © 2010 by Paul Guest. All rights reserved. Printed in the United States of America. No part of this book may be used or reproduced in any manner whatsoever without written permission except in the case of brief quotations embodied in critical articles and reviews. For information, address HarperCollins Publishers, 10 East 53rd Street, New York, NY 10022.

HarperCollins books may be purchased for educational, business, or sales promotional use. For information, please write: Special Markets Department, HarperCollins Publishers, 10 East 53rd Street, New York, NY 10022.

FIRST EDITION

Designed by Mary Austin Speaker

Photograph in frontispiece by Kramer O'Neill

Library of Congress Cataloging-in-Publication Data has been applied for.

ISBN: 978-0-06-168517-0

10 11 12 13 14   OV/RRD   10 9 8 7 6 5 4 3 2 1

For June,
This book, this beginning

PROLOGUE

I leaned in over it, my face low to the ground, to the thing I'd broken, the cheap firecracker I'd unraveled from its dry, crumbling mates, its fuse gray, unassuming. I'd snapped it in two so that the powder spilled from it. The firecracker was stolen, as was the lighter: my grandfather kept a bucket of them atop the freezer. If it was ever empty, and it rarely was, my grandmother would shell peas into it, wordless and stroke-daft, her fingers shedding beans into the bucket with ease. But, mostly, this pot held firecrackers my grandfather loved: Black Cats and M-80s and spindly bottle rockets he would light in his hand, only to let go in the seconds before detonation.

Somehow I had discovered the powder inside the firecrackers would not necessarily explode. That it would spark up and shower the ground with a few seconds of flinty fire. I would bend the firecracker into a V-shape, its rupture pointing up, prop it on a piece of dusty gravel so that it stayed that way, and snap my grandfather's stolen fire alive in my hand.

It did not always catch. Some of the firecrackers were old, years old, I think, dry as a mummy. I'd try again, until the fire took hold and the shower of sparks hissed up. It never lasted long. A few seconds. Mostly a smoke that was dense and bitter. But the sparks were starry, amazing to me, bouncing away, obliterated within seconds.

At my grandparents' home there was access to fire: lighters, matches, gasoline, and addled, inconstant supervision. I could do anything.

At night I would stay awake, long past my grandparents' bedtime, just so I could wade through the clotted waters of pay cable, flipping through each channel filled with Chuck Norris movies, cheap junk, and worse. I felt as though each film, vile, barely competent, was meant for no one but me. And in that cathode flicker I grew to love a kind of solitude.

The fire wouldn't catch, wouldn't take. I'd burned my thumb, trying. It felt raw, throbbed. I was on my bare knees now, kneeling on the beat-up driveway. It was summer, the cicadas in the trees singing their buzz saw song.

One last time, I said to myself, flicking the lighter's serrated wheel. Click. Fire. I held it to the broken Black Cat.

Even in the instant, I think I marveled at it, how a shock wave felt, rolling through the body, through my still outstretched hand.

This time: no spill of stars, no bright sizzle bouncing down the slope of the driveway before blinking out in the long grass.

Only the firecracker exploding, its force pitching through my hand and up my arm, leaving it all to tingle and throb, numb meat.

All my fingers were there, though indistinct to me, and I wasn't burned, but even so, I seemed submerged, my ears stuffed with thunder. They rang so sharply it scared me.

I went inside, to a sink, and filled a glass with cold water. This seemed important, the way people on TV are always given water to drink after some barely averted disaster, burning wreckage all around, maybe, but a glass of water, one thousand sips. I drank it all down, still deafened, my ears crammed with struck tuning forks, it seemed. Am I deaf now? I wondered, unsettled, afraid.

The thought was too much. I lay down in my uncle's old bed, high off the floor, in the room he'd left behind for marriage. In one corner a fish tank burbled thickly, the water all algae, all waste, all green neglect.

The ceiling swam above me and I only wanted sleep.

chapter

The night before I broke the third and fourth vertebrae of my neck, I lay in bed imagining what it would be like if that ever happened to me. If there would be pain. If I would die. I was twelve years old. My mother had checked out a book called *Joni* from our Methodist church's sparse library, giving it to me when she finished. I had ignored it for months, choosing instead the tattered Hardy Boys mysteries I loved, the comic books I kept in a cardboard box, or magazines like *BMX Action*. But that night, after my parents had put the newborn twins, Bo and Clay, down for sleep, after my seven-year-old brother, Chan, had gone to his own room upstairs, I turned to the book, thumbing through it. The story of a teenage girl who was paralyzed in a diving accident gripped me, at first, the way cheap horror movies on late-night cable did: the suffering seemed fiction. But when she wrote of awakening in a cold green room, her body naked except for a sheet that covered the body she no longer could feel or move, I could barely stand to read more. As the sheet began to slip away from her and onto the floor, revealing her breasts, her nipples prickling in the cold air, shame scalded her, and I put the book away. I didn't sleep for a while.

The next morning I woke early and dressed, excited. The day before I had graduated from the sixth grade, walking across an old stage in my school's cafeteria to receive my diploma. I was excited because one of my teachers had invited me to her home for a graduation party. Her name was Jody Benson and I had been her student since the first grade. Dark-haired, young, she had come to my classroom, asking for me before leading me to a room in the oldest wing of the school. The room smelled like old books, like binding glue and dust. The floors were wood, and high windows let in light that scarcely seemed to fall to where I stood beside a desk. She asked me to sit and placed a book on an easel before me.

"I've brought you here to test your reading skills," she said, smiling. "Do you know what I mean by that?"

I nodded. I had learned to read early, before beginning kindergarten. As a child, I'd demanded my mother read book after book, over and over again. Neither of my parents had attended college, marrying soon after graduating from high school. My father managed a grocery store in a local chain, having worked in the business since his early teens, and my mother claimed to hate school, to see no sense in most of it, all the while pushing us to do our best. I tried.

"OK, then. We'll start off with easy words, words you won't have any problem with, and go from there."

The book was spiral-bound across the top edge of each page, designed to be flipped over. We began with words, then passages of text. They were easier for me than what I was reading at home. Books about the space shuttle, a history of the robot, mysteries, comic books—almost anything that I could find I opened up. Designed to measure a child's vocabulary, her book grew ever more dense each time she flipped a thick, time-stained page.

After a while, Jody stopped, putting down the pen she had been making notes with. "We can stop there. You've read plenty."

I was disappointed about not finishing. "I can keep going. It hasn't been hard at all." I wanted to please her. To impress her. I knew who she was and the classes she taught. I wanted to be a part of them, to be recognized, to feel special.

Jody looked at me carefully, trying not to smile. After a moment, she flipped the page and picked up her pen. She motioned for me to continue reading. I didn't stop until the book did.

■

At Jody's house I found my best friend, Adam, waiting for me on the back porch. Jody was beginning to grill burgers and hot dogs. Inside, Christina, Gwendy, Missy, Lana, and Michelle, the other members of our gifted class, were playing with Jody's newborn baby daughter. Adam and I were not much interested in that, sitting stoically on the bench while Jody cooked for us. Before long we grew bored, antsy, unwilling to join the girls inside. For five years, we had been the only boys in the class and Jody knew well how much we loved bicycles, riding, racing. She asked if we would like to borrow her and her husband's bicycles until the food was ready. We jumped up, running to the garage.

I should have been wary. An adult would have known better than to ride those bikes. Leaned against the wall, festooned with cobwebs, skinned in dust, the ten-speed bikes had not been used in quite some time. Adam took the first and pedaled a few feet forward, stopping. The tires were flat. I looked down to see that mine were flat, too. Back inside the garage, we found a pump hanging on the wall. Adam inflated his tires quickly and then was gone. I began pumping mine back up.

I climbed atop the bike, feeling awkward from leaning out over the handlebars. All my life I had ridden single-speed bikes with twenty-inch wheels, dirt bikes, BMX bikes with lightweight steel frames. I felt unsafe but pedaled on slowly.

Jody's house sat at the top of a long, steep driveway. To

either side, green lawns sloped down to the road. I didn't see Adam anywhere ahead. Already I was afraid I would wreck. The bike was getting away from me as it coasted down the long incline. I squeezed the right caliper handbrake but it was only mush, a sensation I had felt before on my own bike when the brake cable that ran down to the wheel had frayed or torn entirely. It was a problem I could fix myself but not in motion, not then. My fear began to grow.

I was resigned to the inevitability of crashing, and in those few seconds I had before the bike would be dangerously fast I decided it was better to crash on grass than to land on the asphalt.

I steered to the right, not into Jody's lawn but the grass between her yard and her neighbor's. I tried the useless brakes once more. Nothing.

Maybe I can lay it down in the grass, I thought, though I'm not even sure I knew what that meant. I was rolling over the smooth grass, frozen. I never tried to do anything but ride it out.

What I did not know, what I could not see, would be what changed the rest of my life. At the bottom of the slope, a drainage ditch ran beside the road, overgrown with weeds and thick tussocks of grass. I hit the ditch still traveling at speed. I was thrown from the bike, over the handlebars, catapulted, tossed like a human lawn dart into the earth.

I don't remember flying through the air. Not because I lost consciousness, but because my eyes were sealed shut, out of fear. I came to rest like a bag of sand, sliding to a stop some twelve feet away, beside a thin tree.

I could feel nothing, no pain, no sensation, indeed, there seemed to be no body any longer below my neck, which slowly, faintly, began to register the dullest of aches. There is no real way to describe what this felt like, or did not feel like—the sudden, violent abstraction of the body, the brain left to believe all has vanished in a terrible, surgical instant.

My head felt like a stone and all that my mind could conjure for me to understand was that the rest of me seemed to float away.

Across my chest, my left arm lay crookedly, the radius snapped. My right arm was pinned beneath me, its wrist broken as well. My breath was labored. Something wet seeped from my nose. It felt like blood. I'd later learn it was spinal fluid.

I began to guess what had happened, though I knew nothing in detail about a broken neck, nothing besides what I had read in the book by Joni Eareckson, though I did not think of that then. Instinctively, I knew I'd broken my neck, that I was badly hurt, that I would not be dusting myself off, catching my breath, wincing over scrapes that would soon grow scabs.

Adam stood over me, out of breath, scared.

"Do you need help?" he asked, his voice high and near to flying apart.

"Yes," I said. "Hurry."

And then I was alone for a minute, maybe two. My breaths were ragged. Above me, a low green branch blocked the blue sky of the last day of May.

Jody quickly came to where I lay, dropping down to her knees, her face scared. I could see Adam and the girls standing in a bunch some distance away.

"Are you OK?" she asked, her voice strange.

"I think I've hurt myself," I said, scared to say more.

By then her next-door neighbors had arrived, having seen the accident from their porch. A burly, middle-aged man squatted beside me.

"You OK, buddy? You took quite a spill there."

His voice was better than Jody's, more calm, pitched to comfort me. He placed his hand on my shoulder. I couldn't feel it.

"We're gonna get you up from here, OK? You've knocked the breath out of yourself. We're going to get you up, OK?"

I knew enough to know that I shouldn't be moved. I asked him not to move me, I begged him, but he lifted me easily in his arms, carrying me a few feet back from where I had come to rest after the wreck.

Someone else, another man, maybe his son, helped him stand me up, one of them on each side of me. They must have expected me to shake it off, to get over the scare, to stand on my own. They withdrew some of their support. My knees buckled. I dropped. My head fell over, like a flower on a broken stem. My cheek rested against my chest grotesquely. Without saying another word they softly laid me on the grass again.

I have no idea, no way of knowing, if this ill-advised movement made my injury worse, if the extent of my paralysis grew from any additional trauma. Before the men moved me, took me up in their arms, that fear lit up inside me: that further harm would happen to me if I were so much as touched. But a child is helpless when hurt, when no one really knows what the gravity of permanence feels like, and so it happened and then could not be undone. And in that awful moment, it became no different than the wreck itself, a terrible extension of it. In the time to come, when therapy and surgeries loomed, I put it out of my mind, one more event over which I had no control, not when it happened, and not in the drear, untouchable past. Doctors could only speculate softly: *no way to know, the damage was probably already done.* My parents spoke of it, if they did at all, in terms which minimized or negated any possible effect, but I could hear in my father's voice, beneath it, choked anger, brokenhearted and immense, inconsolable.

The paramedics carefully slipped a hard collar around my neck, a body board beneath me, all to stabilize whatever might be broken or injured. They lifted me into the ambulance and sped away. The paramedic seated beside me, monitoring my vital signs, spoke calmly, reassuringly for a few moments. He mentioned that he had gone to high school with my mother and her brothers, that they had played together as children. He radioed ahead to the hospital.

Probable cervical injury, I heard him quietly say. I don't believe I knew the meaning of *cervical* then, but I understood it intuitively, and fear began to take greater hold within me. I began to feel a permanence rolling over me like a wave, that this injury might not be something that would heal in its own good time. I stared up at the roof of the speeding ambulance, listening to the clatter of things jostling in their drawers and the siren wailing through our passage.

The opening of ambulance doors is a curiously fraught moment: the world outside may never again be as it was. There is a certain staginess about it, a level of focus, from which all one wants to do is hide. By now I wanted it all to be a dream.

My clothes had been cut from me, yellow shorts and a yellow shirt, razored away with no regard to possession. I had no idea this happened, that I lay in the rolling, swaying bay of the ambulance with nothing on. I could feel nothing, and an oxygen mask hissed against my face. I couldn't move. The entire world was a vague sensation of speed, a muffled siren, the practiced calm of a paramedic's voice. Sometime later, in the hospital, while my mother waited in the hallway, a paramedic handed her my shredded clothes in a plastic bag.

■

When the doors opened, the summer light, the humid air spilled in. I blinked reflexively, over and over again. I could see doctors and nurses in their scrubs, waiting. I could see my mother. We lived closer to the hospital than to Jody's home and she had arrived minutes before the ambulance. Jody had called my mother, saying there had been an accident, that it looked like I'd broken one of my arms, that they were going to get me into her car and drive me to the hospital. My mother insisted on the ambulance.

They lifted me out, quickly rolling me inside the emergency room. The ceiling ran above me, down one hallway and another. I was transferred from the stretcher to an examination table. A doctor began to look me over, asking me questions, my name, where I lived, what happened, if I could remember any of it. He shined a penlight into my eyes, asking me not to blink, to follow his hands. Before long I would be whisked away again, and there in the hall my mother and father waited. I began to cry.

"I want to go to sleep, please let me go to sleep," I pleaded. If I could sleep, then maybe this was not real, a nightmare. Maybe I was not injured so badly. Maybe I would awake to, at most, a broken arm, a body that remembered pain, could move once more. That was my desperate, impossible hope.

My father walked beside me briskly, as I was sped toward more intense examination. "You can't do that," he said. "Not now. You have to be brave. You have to let them help you.

Stay awake, let the doctors look at you. You can do that, can't you?"

If he thought I was only scared, or if he feared I had sustained a head injury, that I was slipping off into unconsciousness, I don't know.

I was taken to a freezing room, dimly lit, and lifted onto another table. A doctor removed the collar stabilizing my neck. The faintest hint of pain, like a fever almost but stranger, less apparent, ringed my throat. The doctor looked down at me, speaking calmly, his voice insistent, grave.

"You must be perfectly still now. Whatever you do, you cannot move your head, or your neck. Do you understand, Paul?"

I looked up at him and after a moment said yes.

A woman's voice spoke, disembodied, tinny. The table I was laid upon began to recede, sliding back into the body-long tube of an MRI scanner. I'd never been claustrophobic before, but inside that cramped machine I felt the wild stirrings of panic. Whatever calm I'd managed to hold fast to began to slip away. I rocked my head from side to side, wanting out, begging to be let out. I knew this was no good, that I could hurt myself even further, thrashing about, but that only meant that I understood a simple, mortal fact, not that I could stand it without terror. Was this less harmful than being stood, than that blind, dumb courtesy of an hour ago? I didn't know. I couldn't stop. This at last was too much.

A man's voice buzzed from speakers which seemed to be placed inside the machine. An odd mixture of tones played through his speech: wan sympathy, boredom, an air of command. *Be still*, he said. *Be still.*

I held my breath. The scanner began its clatter, dowsing me in a magnetic field which would reveal an image of what I'd broken, the unseen wounds.

An endless, watchful stream of nurses marked my first night: vital statistics were measured, my temperature taken, sleep always interrupted. I wanted sleep, I'd said, the blinding occlusion of dreams, a world in which I was still tethered to my life. My old life. I wanted my room at home and the bed which was ancient and looked it: bent nails in the battered wood were hammered back in. How old it was, where it came from, to whom it had belonged a long time ago, are details in stories I can't remember, or was never told. Now it had passed out of my life forever. Now I slept, or tried to, in an intensive care electric hospital bed, which would raise and lower and had chrome rails along its whole length; the mattress was dense, sealed in vinyl to protect against incontinence. I wore a child's diaper.

The following nine days fade into the blur of trauma: much of the time, I was sick, unable to eat or keep water down. I sucked ice chips from a paper cup, a few at a time: nurses rationed them, afraid too much would stir up the nausea which sloshed in my stomach all the time. I still felt nothing below my neck, less than nothing. I felt hot, burning up, yet I couldn't feel temperature at all. The rest of me had become a blankness, a screen upon which my nervous system attempted to project a self which no longer existed and with every insensate day grew more remote.

My parents took turns sleeping in the room, waking up wild-haired and bleary-eyed. My father was thirty-one, my mother thirty, both of them younger than I am now.

Relatives orbited during visitation hours, full of scattershot encouragement, half understanding my diagnosis. I stayed in bed, miserable, bored, scared, waiting for something to happen, to change. I could hardly sit up in bed without the room spinning, my blood thudding through my head, vertigo swamping me. The television anchored to the wall bleated all day.

By degrees I could sit upright again after a few days had passed, though I felt little better. Doctors came and went, and their demeanor became a kind of running commentary: one seemed kind and one arrogant, abrasive, indifferent; others were good-humored, encouraging. All spoke to me mostly of the present and recent past: this had happened to me, and this was now happening to me. Their words deftly dodged the impending future, speaking to my parents the hard words, the final ones, that I wouldn't walk again.

Soon I could be pushed around the hospital floor in a wheelchair. I was grateful, even for this little change in surroundings. The hallway walls were painted with aggressive cheer. Animals gamboled about in primary colors. A boy pedaled a bicycle made of paint. Pushed for short walks around the floor, I would dread the turn that revealed him, all his danger.

It seemed like a long time had passed, that this was my life and always had been. The days settled into peculiar rhythms, the space between catastrophe and convalescence, which hadn't even begun. Inside my body still were two fractured vertebrae, a bruised and swollen spinal cord, and in each arm a bone knitting crookedly. I couldn't exist this way forever, without decisive treatment, rehabilitation, and my parents knew this, investigating as best they could available options, but keeping their efforts largely secret from me. I could scarcely imagine what one day would be like, let alone the prospect of leaving, transferring to another hospital in another city. I had become more stable now and though I didn't speak of it, I knew this waiting could not last long.

And it didn't. I can't remember a single distinguishable thing about the man, but when a doctor entered my room the morning of the fifth day, carefully, looking first to each of my stricken parents, I knew that whatever he had to say could not be good. Lying on my left side, facing the door, I wanted to shrink away, to vanish.

The doctor pulled a chair close to the bed, sat down. He spoke.

"Paul, it's time that we talked about some things. Hard things. I'll come right out and say it: you bruised your spinal cord severely. That much you already know. It's not what we call a complete injury. The cord wasn't severed. You're lucky. But, even so, the chances are great, they are overwhelming, that you won't be able to walk again. You might regain some function. Your arms, maybe, your fingers. A leg. You might not. We don't know. In a few days, you and your parents will make some important choices about how and where you'll begin therapy. But you will be in a wheelchair the rest of your life."

My parents, listening, stricken, seemed to bristle. The air felt like the prelude to thunder.

I made a bad joke: "Would I still be able to play the piano?" I knew that it was a clichéd trope of rehabilitation narratives, or a joke my father might make, but it was the only thing I could think of. I didn't feel like laughing. Or crying. I felt flattened. Drained. Acutely aware of my parents' anguish. Their grief was worse than mine, more immediate, crushing and unbearable, and through them I could better see, more deeply understand how radically changed the rest of my life would be.

I was twelve years old. A quadriplegic. I barely knew the word's meaning.

chapter

My neck was always a misery. Not because of pain from the injury. The collar was oppressively hot, designed to immobilize the neck: made of two stiff halves, each wrapped in a bandage-like sleeve, they locked together at each side. Beneath the chin was a hard shelf, shaped generally like the lines of one's jaw. When snapped together, both pieces held the neck and head still. They also held in the body's heat, like an infernal scarf, one which could not be removed. My skin there broke out in rashes, itched, and there was no relief that was not dangerous. I loved the lenient nurses who knew pity and would open the collar at night, for just a brief while, the air an ambient balm. They'd dust the inflamed skin with baby powder and let me sleep that way, if only for a few hours.

My broken arms were splinted; more decisive treatment like casts would wait until we knew more about my prognosis. Whatever irritation they must have caused the skin of my arms was lost, unfelt. But I could feel, heavy across my chest, a weight which would never move: that of my left arm, rising and falling with each breath. And, yet, my left arm rested at my side, motionless like a dead thing, and nothing which truly touched the bare skin of my chest, no stethoscope or cold pearl of water, cut through the implacable numbness. It was maddening, the certainty that my arm was right there, as if I were resting, when it was plainly elsewhere. I think I had heard of the neurological phenomenon of phantom pain, or read of it in one of the sodden encyclopedias I thumbed through at night, but I was too young then to be calm, to wait on the trauma within me to draw back, even a little. I fretted over that imaginary limb, simultaneously wanting it to go away and hoping, ever so faintly, that it was my arm, in spite of what I could see. To feel a thing then, when so much of my body had vanished from perception, to feel anything at all was a hope, a dangerous, illogical one, but hope all the same.

For the first nine days, marked by dread and not time, I can remember this much. I had been plagued by nausea the whole time: everything was heat, too much of it—temperature regulation, digestion, everything was affected, directly or otherwise, by the accident. Time would calm it all, but until then, when the newness of the trauma faded, I could only boil and suffer. It was strange to feel so little yet still be affected by it all: if my body below the level of the bruised spinal cord was in no way apparent to me, it was still there, unharmed, untouched, subject to every stimulus it had always known. And so I was, in a way, two parts of one whole, divided but inextricably linked, no matter the numbness.

My stomach still roiled and it was hard to keep anything down. Late one night, a doctor came to my bedside, leaning over me, his hands knotted together. He seemed vexed, not quite ready to say anything. Used to the look, I waited. Then he began.

"The acids in your stomach, Paul, because of everything you're going through, it's like your body, everything about it, is upset. That's why you feel so nauseous all the time. We're going to treat that by putting a tube into your nose and down into your stomach, so we can give you medicine, OK?"

When he walked away, I felt something begin to give way inside me. Up until then, I'd faced more misery and indignity than I would have thought possible. I lay there, numb and sick in a diaper, helpless. It was too much to bear, too frightening, a last invasion I could experience and not break, utterly. When he returned with nurses, I was already sobbing.

Anyone so limited could hardly fight, but I tried. I tried. The neck collar prevented much movement, and any was dangerous, but I turned my head side to side, just slightly, a pitiful, unacceptable range. Fat tears rolled down my face like marbles. I begged them all, *no, no, no, please, no.*

"Hold him, hold him still," the doctor said. Nurses gripped my head on either side.

From a sterile pack, the doctor fished out a long transparent tube and dabbed its head in a clear lubricant. He paused almost as if to warn me but then said nothing.

Then the tube entered one nostril, its gauge slight enough to pass through, down my throat and into my stomach. I couldn't thrash or resist. I could only relent. To the pain, the discomfort, but most distressingly the feeling of powerlessness, of violation. It was in that moment, I think, the weight of everything which had happened fell upon me, undeniably, and the knowledge of it crushed me.

When the phone rang I was sick. Fevered. A bladder infection, the nurse said. Nothing serious but it frightened me. I wanted to speak to whoever had called. It was Billy Stevens, a brash kid, smart-mouthed, poor. He sat beside me in math, pelting others with spitballs, expert at disdain. I said hello. They were laughing, whoever was with him, giggling in the background. Whatever was so funny, neither let on, snickering between their attempts to show concern for me.

The call ended, and I had no idea what had been so riotous, but in my bed the mystery was funny, was more than that: a momentary touch of the strangeness of childhood. I barely knew them and would never see them again, but that they called was a kindness greater than many of my closer friends ever managed.

I was ill but for a moment I was not in critical condition.

Those first ten days were not all misery, not quite. I was cheerful, optimistic, though scared. I was often uncomfortable, hot, weak, unable to sleep well or much at all, but I was in no great amount of pain for the most part. I could still feel nothing below my neck; my body, all its muscles, seemed to have fallen into a deep, deep sleep.

One evening my uncle Randy, my mother's oldest brother, came to visit. He ran the family business, the junkyard their father had begun. He was short, with a bristled little mustache, and hair that had turned gray before he'd left high school far behind. We had been close, even though he was eccentric, with a wild temper, given to chewing the collars of his shirts in his just barely sublimated rages. Anything could set him off, but his fits, and their profane squalls, were so frequent, so repressed, he was nothing to fear, an impotent oddball who spent his days covered in grease, pulling odd parts from the rusted husks of wreckage which piled up beneath tall pines.

"Little buddy," he said, his voice full of his usual bluster, his pithy down-home inanities, but now rang hollow, more like a question, what you might say to a dimly recalled, half-recognized relative. This wasn't lost on me, lying there in a diaper, immobilized, watching the ceiling's changeless face.

"Little buddy, you need to close your eyes a second, we brought you something. A surprise."

I felt like I knew what it would be, and my heart caved in a little bit further. I smiled, my eyes drawn shut.

"Pistol," he said. It was the way he talked, faux cornpone punctuating gaps between apoplectic bouts of cursing.

When I opened my eyes, Randy stood at the foot of the bed with a new bicycle, gleaming chrome even in the hospital's wan, institutional light. He'd lifted it up into the bed, holding it upright. It was expensive, the kind of bike I had lingered over a long, long time in bicycle shops and in the glossy magazines I used to thumb through in grocery stores. Long before my accident, and long before this moment, I had loved that bike. For all its iridescent unattainability. For its perfection. And I loved it then. I loved it then as I loved my old life, and mourned them both. In the small hospital room there was no room for a bike. No room for a useless reminder. My parents carried it home, hung it in a closet on hooks, its fate not so different from Jody's ten-speed, to be forgotten in the dust.

■

A week had passed since the accident. Nothing in my body had moved. No twitch of toe or flex of knee. Except for when I slept, the television was constant motion and babble, its fuzzy picture rolling pablum. Visitors brought videocassettes for me to watch: bad comedies, bad action flicks. Everything was cheap, shoddy. I nodded off, in and out, sometimes absorbed, and other times, pressed by boredom, anxiety. I was not particularly transported by Arnold Schwarzenegger's *Commando*, none of its slapdash gore, when my leg moved, drawing up almost to my chest, the muscles beneath the white hospital sheets trembling, then extending back to where it had been, motionless, for so much time.

I had not been able to move in days. Or felt anything but the ghost of my arm fading away, now hardly noticeable. My mother, reading beside the bed, looked over, shocked. Whatever hope I'd nursed, it had been small and inconstant, not crumbling but receding. To see my leg move again, after everything, was frightening. Why was this happening? And how, in its inexplicability, could it be good?

Her books slid from her lap onto the floor. Her face composed itself like rapid questions, and tears welled in her tired eyes. "That will show them," she said. "They don't know everything."

Later in the day, a doctor on his rounds explained the spasm was not all that surprising, common, even, in injuries like mine, since the swelling of the spinal cord would eventually subside. He cautioned that the movement was no indication that my injury might be less severe than initially thought. Much of the nervous system, the spinal cord, the nerves which threaded out from it, the sentinel brain atop it all, was still a mystery, not subject to reliable predictions. Still, with every conversation I held with neurologists, orthopedic surgeons, urologists, nurses, and more, I came to a secondhand knowledge of the body's workings which had been before only abstract, the stuff of textbook diagrams and lesson plans. Now, I was the lesson, I was the studied body, and even in that terrible state, I couldn't help but be queasily fascinated, the way one looks over the edge of a high building, the world plummeting away.

By the end of my stay, I had been diagnosed and stabilized, no longer gripped in the whirl of vertigo if I tried to sit upright. I could drink and eat without my digestive system rejecting everything. One leg had even moved. My doctors in concert with my parents began preparing me for the decisions to come, when I'd be transferred to an adequate rehabilitation center. The thought of flying off to Denver, where the venerable Craig Hospital was located, was equally terrifying and thrilling: I had never traveled farther from home than Florida. At night, with my mother and father, we talked about what it might be like and how they'd visit. But Denver was not our only, or perhaps even best, option.

In Atlanta, less than two hours away, a city I knew, where relatives lived on streets crowded with magnolias and dogwoods, was Shepherd Spinal Center, a newer rehabilitation hospital, one exclusively focused on treating spinal cord injuries.

Unknown to me, my father had toured its three small patient floors and its gymnasiums where physical therapists stretched limbs and tried to strengthen flagging muscles. He was holding a packet of information given to him during his visit. Inside were the standard narratives, the smiling faces, plausibly vague assurances. He showed some of it to me.

"This is where you'll be going," he said. "Your mother and I decided this was best. That we'd be close enough to visit. Every weekend. It's not even two hours away."

I can't say that I chose to be transferred to Atlanta, to Shepherd; the decision was too large, too crucial, for a child to make. When my parents told me I'd be going there, it was the night before I would have to leave by medical transport, an ambulance, and though I felt small, too small to even cry or feel much fear, unexpected relief opened up inside me. Ten days had passed since my accident, during which I'd slept little, was often unable to eat. I'd been forced to consider a changed life before I even knew what a life could fully become.

chapter

THREE

When I left Chattanooga behind, the ambulance drove slowly over interstate rumble. I was lightly sedated and slept all the way. In their station wagon, my parents trailed behind. I had no particular vision of where I was going, what it might look like, or even what might happen to me. Physical therapy, yes, which had been given to me sparingly in Chattanooga, but before it could in earnest begin at Shepherd, I knew surgery on my spine might wait for me. I knew this only as an abstraction: I had worried at its possibility all along, its potential for pain, the inescapable fear that something could go wrong. Over all this, I'd fretted silently, during the long days and nights, and when the doors of my second ambulance opened in Atlanta, the stretcher that held me was rolled out and into the lobby, where elevators opened like mouths.

A space in a room on the third floor was reserved for me. Quickly transferred from the stretcher into the hospital bed, identical to what I'd had in Chattanooga, and identical to the one I'd sleep in, alone, for twenty-three years, I waited. And waited. My parents had found their way before long, sitting in wooden chairs at my side. My father chatted idly, rambling as he did when nervous, and my mother nervously pushed errant, oily hair from my forehead. I hadn't showered in ten days, no more than sponge baths, not since the night before breaking my neck.

Nurses circulated in and out of the room, recording vital signs, giving papers to my parents, speaking to me, looking at me hard, taking quick measure. No one said very much. I was now in a triage-style suite sectioned into four living spaces separated by ceiling to floor curtains. A little television on an adjustable arm hung from the ceiling. I had one small closet and no desk space. It held the two essential items of my life: a bed and a wheelchair. Anything more was incidental.

My mother began tacking get well cards and pictures of family to the wall. She hung my few clothes. My father talked about weather, traffic, all the cars running down Peachtree. After some time, he trailed away, stood up, and asked if we wanted something from a vending machine.

■

This is the narrative of convalescence. How it begins. It is familiar to anyone who has stumbled into its uncertain stream: nothing you can say has much weight. Every word is spoken across a distance. The moment you become ill, the instant injury divides you from your life, from the world, from the ones you love and who in return love you, you are floating away from everything and everyone, on numbing ice, desperate for some vestiges of consolation.

The suite was fully occupied by three other patients, though now it was empty. Only us. Outside the room and down the hallway, towards the nursing desk, were the gymnasiums filled with raised mats and modified exercise equipment. I could hear the grunts of effort and the clack and whir of electric machinery, wheelchairs coursing about, and the gauzy whoosh of respirators. Moans, too, floated down the hallway, ghostly, full of pain. We ignored it all, waiting.

First to enter the room was the man who slept across from me. Older, past his middle years, with white hair that stood coarsely up from a pink scalp, he pushed along his wheelchair with wheels that had pegged spokes; his hands were curves, claws, his fingers paralyzed. He pressed against each peg with his palm and slowly went. A nurse walked behind him, pushing lightly. The man had no strength in him and no words, either. He went to bed, where much of the time he'd stay, his skin plagued by sores that would not heal. Before long, I'd learn the currency of that sad realm was the story of your injury, what happened to you and how and why and every other detail in forensic completeness. I'd learn that he, his first name Forrest, had fallen into a pit on land he owned, pitched headfirst, alone, undiscovered a long time. He seemed bewildered, lost, overcome by the change in his life, unable to accept it, to ever live again. When I heard, years later, that he hadn't lived long, had put his gun to his temple and ended it, I wasn't shocked.

The next, and most significant patient to my time at Shepherd, to enter the room was Josh Anderson, seventeen years old and nearly seven feet tall, all arms and legs and Albany, New York, accent. So lanky he barely fit in a wheelchair, his knees pushed high up, and his arms nearly could reach the floor. As ungainly an experience as disability is, it must have been impossible to be him, to inhabit a body which had been made for basketball, which he had played, to push against the ordinary limits of all the accommodations the world makes for the disabled. His bed required an extension, else his feet hung from the bed. His chair would need to be custom designed, stretched out, stronger than the usual chair and lighter, too. He fascinated me: the five years' age difference, his accent, and his body which was not so affected as mine. Above the protrusion of his larynx, a white crescent scar stood out, rising and falling when he spoke. I wanted to be his friend, I needed to be his friend, before we had even met. My parents would soon leave, forced to return to jobs and younger children, promising weekend visits. Soon and very soon.

Josh could push himself around and came over to us, gliding to a stop. He introduced himself. His voice rang in that awkward register of adolescence. He was funny, kind.

"You'll like it here," he assured me. To my parents, he said, "Don't worry, I'll look out for him."

A teenager's boast, sure, but at that time, it was something to hold on to, and it meant all the world.

Here, there was no hesitation. Here, the holding pattern my life had been in ceased and I was immersed in the reality of my rehabilitation. Both broken arms were quickly put into casts. The collar that had supported my broken neck was only a temporary fix. A dangerous one, in that it really didn't fix anything. It was time to consider real treatment, which primarily meant surgery, in which my vertebrae would be fused using a graft of bone chiseled away from my hip. The disc between the vertebrae would be removed, making room for the hip bone and screws or wiring to hold it all in place. The surgery was painful, invasive, but one other option existed.

That option was to place me in a fiberglass vest, lined with lamb's wool, with four steel bars connected to a metal ring around my head. That ring would be bolted with fierce inch-long screws into my skull at each temple and in cor-

responding positions at the back of my head. The effect of
the contraption is to completely immobilize the spine in its
correct alignment so that any damage may heal. The halo, as
it's called for the ring, is a gamble of sorts, hoping the body
is able to heal the vertebrae naturally.

Maybe because it was the best choice, or maybe because
I was so young, my body barely touched by the hammer
stroke of puberty, the halo was bolted into my head soon
after I arrived. I'd live this way for eight weeks at least. Most
patients underwent the process while awake, the sites for
the screws deadened by local anesthetic. The thought horrified me, the imagined sensation of four thumb-long bolts
being turned, crank by audible crank, steel into bone.

But an X-ray spared me.

My left arm had begun to knit crookedly and would have
to be rebroken, set again, a plate screwed into the radius, the
bone running down to the thumb. This surgery would be
performed and then the halo fastened to me. I would be
under general anesthesia.

The operating room was cold and green and everything else
was bright. In an anteroom I waited with soft music drift-
ing down like blandness itself. Curtains circled me. When
a woman came to my side, wrapped in scrubs, her mouth
covered with a mask, I was grateful.

She pressed a latch at the bottom of the intravenous bag hanging over me like a transparent cloud.

"Can you count backwards from one hundred for me, sugar?"

"One hundred . . . ninety-nine . . . ninety-eight . . ."

All the sound in the room went weird, like it had shape, and then that shape was turning fluid, running out of mind like molten wax. I was gone.

When they rolled my sleeping body from recovery, my mother saw slender threads of blood running back from my temples into my hair, to dry unseen.

When sensation began to return to my body, it was late at night, and in bed I was watching television. All lights out. Volume low. Johnny Carson. It felt like water on my chest, a dew on the skin above my sternum evaporating into the air. No warning had preceded it. No hint. One moment there was only the numbness that had been absolute and un-changing. And then, a tingling like I had come inside from a storm, soaked to the bone, beginning to dry.

I rang the nurse's desk by blowing into a tube, which activated a blinking light on an intercom. It spoke after a moment, bad sound, cheap and fuzzy.

"Well, what do you need?"

It was Beaver, a middle-aged man who always worked in the darkness of third shift. His manner was librarial, hushed voice cramming all his syllables up so that they uncoiled from his mouth. Someone who didn't particularly crave the company of anybody else. At night, when it was your time to be turned from one side to the other, or to take medicine, you would wake to find his lined face floating in the gloom above your bed.

I asked him to come to the room. That I needed something. After a long, querulous silence, the blinking intercom light went dark.

And there he was in the dark, looking put out, ill used. He snapped on a lamp and crossed his arms.

"Well, what do you need?"

It was what he always said. Almost the only thing he said. To Beaver, the world was a chain of incessant demand.

"I think I can feel something for the first time. Again. I mean, since my accident."

"Where?" he asked, his voice now curious.

"On my chest. All across the top part of my chest, like a line."

"Hmm," he said. He fished a ballpoint pen from his shirt pocket. "Close your eyes. Don't open them. Don't peek. Don't waste my time."

I closed my eyes. I waited. I waited.

"What do you feel?" Beaver asked.

"Nothing."

"Now what do you feel?"

"Nothing."

"That's good. And now."

And there it was, the cold tip of the pen running across my skin. It traced through the water feel, a straight line through what had long been blankness.

"The tip of the pen. In a straight line, left to right."

Beaver didn't say anything for a moment. Then I felt the pen pressing into my chest, not like I'd always felt, not like normal. Less apparent but there. *There.*

"The pen. Not moving. Right?"

I opened my eyes. Beaver was slipping the pen back into his breast pocket. His face gave no hint of what he thought.

"Yep. Right. Congratulations. Go back to sleep."

He dimmed the lamp and left me there in the darkness. The strange feel of water persisted, tingling, pooling up, a mystery.

Doctors always came by too early. In chatty packs, thick clutches of patient records in their arms. Most days I waited for them, already awakened by the sunlight that came through the wall-length windows and metal slats which did little but hang there. We'd perform our perfunctory exchanges, pleasantries, good-morning-and-did-you-sleep-wells, before settling into what one of them called "the brass tacks." They would look me over, take blood pressure if a nurse had not yet been by to do so, peer at the urine which had collected overnight in a bag hanging from the bed frame. In it, they scanned for signs of blood, darkness, sediment. Last was usually close inspection of the halo jacket I wore, checking the skin underneath the fiberglass vest for signs of rash or irritation or infection. With cotton swabs, they probed the sites where the halo was bolted into my skull, applying Betadine, a muddy red disinfectant, and some days produced torque wrenches to tighten the bolts. The sensation was sickening more than painful, and on those days I dreaded the weirdness of it.

But the morning after Beaver had dragged a pen over my skin, there were more of them than was usual. One of them spoke.

"We hear there might be some changes going on in here."

I said yes.

"Mind if we take a look?"

Even if I did mind, I had no power to stop them, or anyone, from putting their hands on me. Disability isn't so much about the loss of control as it is about the transferal of it. From yourself to someone else, to loved ones, strangers. To devices.

Sure, I nodded.

He brought out something which looked like a small wheeled pizza cutter. On the wheel were pins of varying sharpness. He flicked it and the wheel spun a bit.

"Where exactly are you feeling something?"

I explained to them, the weird tickle that still was there, just above my sternum. He took the wheel, placed it on my chest, and began to push it across my skin.

"Tell me what you feel," he said. "Sharp, dull, sharp, dull, sharp, sharp, dull, dull. Whatever it seems like to you."

The difference, then, was negligible, barely perceptible. I closed my eyes, trying to concentrate, but it made the sensation no more apparent, just strange, disembodied.

Several minutes passed that way. At best, I was uncertain of any differences, and could only feel the wheel pass over that part of me. The rest of my body was still lost, and even though I'd soon grow to hate that probing, its ephemerality which only grew with your eyes closed, it was cause for hope, a dangerous thing, an untruth not quite uttered.

You enter this place, this junkyard of bodies, where at night the hallways are humid with the vapor of shower water, and the stink of shit, when nurses pass from room to room, their hands ghostly white in latex gloves. You enter this place, more than half dead, wanting to go back out just as you were before, as if this were somehow possible, bearing up in your arms the weight of your old life, carrying it just as you ever had.

You enter this place. You enter this place. And you wait.

For your body, for your nervous system, for the manifold nerves which comprise it, to do something, to do anything, for your faithless skin to pebble with gooseflesh in a draft of cold air, for one muscle out of the six hundred gone slack to convulse back to life, for the most desperate fears within you to recede. And whatever it is you fear, and all of it is elemental, whether you'll walk again or dress yourself or eat without help or, you hardly want to think it, make love, all those fears are not assuaged by your time here. Those fears are systemically stoked. By instruction and by harangue and by slide show and videotape.

You must not become what you most fear.

chapter

"I swear to God," said Gary. "This big. Like a basketball. I looked down and—"

"And what?" I asked, bumping up to one of the tables where meals were served.

Gary, an African-American man in his late forties, had been gone for a couple of days, and no one knew where he had been. Back in his bed and hooked up to an IV, he had recovered enough to join us for breakfast. That morning, his voice sounded even more gruff and abraded than usual. "Never you goddamned mind. You mind your own concerns. That's what you do."

He spoke like that, irascible, profane, and never cared

much for my presence, as young as I was. Gary had almost bled out in a gas station parking lot after being shot by a stranger. The bullet had severed his spinal cord, exiting his body through the back of one of his lungs.

"No, seriously, what?" I asked again. "I wanna know what you guys are talking about."

Seated beside Gary was Josh, all angles, his face mapped by acne. He grinned, amused with Gary, with my confusion. He waved me off. *Later*, he said. *Later*.

Down to the table's end I went, not far from them, feeling sullen and waiting for a nurse who'd feed me dry toast, some grapes, orange juice from concentrate. I could see Josh laughing, his face fixed with a conspiratorial grin. I had no idea what they were talking about. Why I could not hear it.

I suffered no less than any of them, was more acutely affected by my injury than most, in fact, and yet I was the scrawny kid held at a remove, outside real fraternal bond.

"That's not normal," Josh yelped, his eyes wide.

Gary was nonplussed, now stirring his moat of grits with a spoon.

"On a stack of Bibles, my man. On a stack of Bibles."

Later that night, after therapy, when we were in our beds, speaking through the swaying wall of curtain between us, Josh explained to me what elephantiasis was. The thought of Gary's grotesquely swollen testicles was not so hard to countenance: all around me were proofs of frailty. I was one. I thought of my own body swollen that way and a swimmy feeling spilled into my head. It was funny, we laughed, but underneath it all, miniature horror percolated. The body was all difficulty, compromise; it could never be sublime.

As if the malfunctioned fact of our bodies were not lesson enough every day, we were required to attend classes, six weeks of them, during which we mostly watched weird videotapes. A television set and VCR were set up in a lounge, all its furniture removed, for us to herd our wheelchairs into. And then it would begin, the tape viewed so many times, lines ran across the picture like gaps through which all the color had slowly seeped. Each one focused on a particular body system, the bladder, the bowels, whatever now no longer worked all that well. They were awful, without exception, anthropomorphized to the point of absurdity. In one, a poor actor gamboled about in a costume meant to be a bladder, his arms ureters. In another, the long rope of the intestines was portrayed by a sad troupe, bound together in an organ-esque fabric tube, dancing in clumsy lockstep with the rhythms of our disrupted, dysfunctional digestive system.

Worse by far was the slide show of bedsores, in which the color, mercilessly, had not been drained away and blood-red were all the cavities which had opened up in the flesh of anonymous asses. There were the debridements of necrotic tissue and the queasy white flashes of bone. Unseen faces, always. Only what had been ruined by carelessness, depression. One slide lingered on the scalded foot of a man who had not checked the water's temperature before soaking in it. It had boiled liked a pot roast and looked about the same before being amputated.

We left the room, going back out into institutional light, defeated.

I was twelve and sex was an inconstant beacon, and it was impossible, then, to know if its light drew me through the darkness of adolescence to it, whatever that might mean, or whether it was the herald of something unknown, unknowable, tumbling headlong toward me. I was twelve and the youngest patient in the hospital. If anyone might claim childhood still, even in the face of the paralysis we all were afflicted with, it was me. I was a child, twelve years old, expert already in the infinite ways I could be ruined, how I'd set myself at that edge of that blade.

But I hadn't yet learned the end of love. Or, at least, its unlikelihood, its sad truncation. After the videos of our song-and-dance bowels, after the grisly slide shows, a last video remained, transferred from film decades ago, maybe epochs. We were gathered up in the dark one last time to learn the crater impact our injuries would leave in our sex lives. If they persisted. If they were recognizable as such. If our bodies even recognized the neural play of sex.

Barely better than low-rent pornography, the video showed actors who marched lockstep through the lines and the actions and seemed to want this awful thing over. If the video was in any way helpful, with its suggestions of mutual masturbation, with its call to reconsider intimacy and its quiet insistence on the long shadow of loneliness, it wasn't helpful to us, who were silent by the end. Instead, its sullen depictions of the possibilities of sex felt more and more like libidinal hazing.

I just felt numbed, injected by shame. I thought of my mother, Pentecostal and furious, hearing I'd been included in this group. Nobody else moved.

A naked woman, with dark hair vining down her back, stood before her partner in a wheelchair, also naked. She put her arms around his back, like a mighty hug, and began rocking back and forth, trying to lift him up, until they spilled into what looked like a hotel bed. In another scene, she knelt before her partner, seated again, and fumbled with his jeans, fishing out his half-limp penis: she gripped it perfunctorily before taking it in her mouth. Later, back in bed, she straddled his face. There was little sense to the sequence and less that was sexy. Dark mutters ran through the room. The air grew leaden.

"Fuck this," one of us barked, then shoved through the door.

As we began to disperse, we took with us each a share of

that grief, like a latent seed, a weight we'd carry, that would grow.

It was easy to know the most serious ways in which my body had been changed. But time slowly taught the intimacies and embarrassments of the injury. One night I had to lie there, sick to my stomach, on my left side, unable to move. The curtains were pulled and all light extinguished, save one little lamp, clamped to the headboard. The bulb burned bright; the back of my head and neck stung, sang out. And in my head, inside it, pounded a metronome said to be my heart. Each pulse lit little stars in my eyes. I was sick. I wanted to vomit, right there, right there, into the sheets and the soft foam beneath.

A nurse, a grim woman, spoke-limbed, worked behind me. When I moaned she shushed me, pulling from me thick, claylike stool.

"It's like peanut butter," she said.

You begin this in mystery, in confusion. Maybe you have no chance of ever getting better. Maybe you might improve. Maybe one arm begins to function once more and you learn to feed yourself all over again, like a child. Maybe you begin to breathe easier, without mechanical assistance, and slowly you're weaned from the respirator. Maybe not. Maybe the rest of your life will be tethered to that machine, to strangers who care for you by caring for it.

You are the machine. The damaged machine.

After the doctors in the mornings, and after the nurses who come with updated orders for your daily treatment, after you are washed with old rags, and the night's clear issue of urine drained away, you are dressed in soft clothes so your skin won't scratch, won't break down, won't turn to the sores which horrified you. You're sent out to therapy, to be laid out on mats, all the joints turned, all the tendons stretched, all the muscles contracted, by will if you can, or by electrodes buttoned into sponges soaked in brine, placed atop weak areas. The low current tingles and you wait for a reaction.

But this is all waiting. All of it. You wait. And they wait.

To see what will happen, what will change. For that to run its course, to plateau.

The first upwell of sensation, like water evaporating from the skin of my sternum, had begun to spread, down my chest and across to my shoulders. It was easy to miss at first, the way a room at sunrise slowly begins to swell with light. Easy to persist in the numbness to which I'd grown accustomed. And, then, a feather of air, a therapist's hand, water from a rag: all at once, they'd register, at first in disbelief, and then in careful degrees.

In the first few weeks at Shepherd, when my nervous system began to recover from its trauma, I would call home to tell my parents every small change. It felt good to dare hope, it felt good to give them encouragement. A nurse would hold the phone to my ear, after working the receiver through the scaffold of the halo, and dial the number home.

"Hello," my mother would say in the days before the ubiquity of caller ID.

"Hello," I'd say back, a charged moment one never becomes better at managing.

"I have some good news," I'd say. And, whatever that good news was, whether I could feel the ring finger on my left hand, or the pain of a needle sliding into my flesh, I would tell her.

If my father was home from work, he would listen in.

Whenever there was good news, there were also tears. Tears like a second language, tears like the only one.

At first, physical therapy was a passive activity: though I slowly began to feel more and more of my body, and in varying degrees of intensity, no muscle control had returned. Each morning, following breakfast, patients would be transferred onto raised mats by therapists. If the patient could move his arms, he worked at strengthening each muscle:

biceps, triceps, deltoids. If he could move his legs, if his spinal cord had not been severed, he exercised them. I could only lie back, while a therapist fought against the natural tightening of my hamstrings, the contraction of muscles I no longer used; in the distance, a stereo played a local radio. I chatted with the therapist, watched the ceiling, waited for three hours to pass, when we had lunch. The sessions often had the communal striving of an exercise class, and though I was not able to participate in the work, I was glad to be among these people, a part of a large, fragile hope.

At night, late, when the doctors were nowhere to be seen, and nurses moved quietly from room to room, turning patients from one side to the other, to relieve pressure from bony prominences, was the only real time that wasn't regimented. I'd stay up late watching the little television set that swung over my bed, or listening to cassette tapes with headphones. Bill Cosby, Phil Collins, Jimmy Buffett—tapes passed around, a fluid library with materials no better than the collective tastes of the patients. I didn't care. All I wanted was a shadow of privacy.

Soon I could feel both arms, my chest and stomach. And then my legs, like ghosts. The way one might strain to better hear a distant sound, all concentration upon it, ill defined, was akin to how my body began to return to halting operation.

One evening, while the others around me slept, my leg spasmed, drawing up. Once, then twice. A third time. I tried to cause the spasm again. I could. *Neat*, I thought.

The next morning a physical therapist named Steve poked his head through my curtains. When needed, he helped dress patients. Rangy and tall, funny, he was a favorite. I was glad to see him.

"Look what I can do." I yawned, drowsy. My right leg lurched, too stiff after sleep. I tried again. This time, it bent up, an inverted V beneath the sheets. Steve stepped in, sliding the curtains shut again, leaning with both arms on my wheelchair.

"What's that you're doing there?" he drawled casually.

"I can make myself, my leg spasm."

"Let's see that again," he requested, quietly. "Try to see if both will, uh, spasm for you."

Both legs drew slowly up. The left quivered, weaker than the other.

Steve's face was all smile, intensely so, and for a second he was silent, considering me. "What?" I asked, still morning dim, confused.

"Oh, Paul-y," he said, stilling my shaking knee with his large hand. "Paul-y."

■

I could move my legs. Barely. They trembled, a symptom of their weakness, of the muscular atrophy which had already set in, but symptomatic also of the still inflamed spinal cord, which pressed against the inner spinal column, interrupting nerve pathways. Whatever I hadn't ruined back in May was slowly, with the lessening of inflammation, reconnecting the body with the brain. Day by day, it seemed, I improved.

Except for my arms. No, except for one muscle, the deltoid, responsible for lifting the arm away from the body. Without them, nothing else would work. No matter the exercise I tried or the amount of time I spent hooked to machines running electrical current into the muscle, there was no discernible improvement, no increase in strength. No, they slowly atrophied, losing mass, melting away beneath the skin. With time, my shoulders visibly narrowed.

I could operate an electric wheelchair now, guiding it with my right hand. But that was the limit of what I could do with either arm.

The rest of that summer, and for years afterwards, I tried to regain their use, though I knew, but never said, it wouldn't happen. Even so, I was lucky. Luck beyond luck gilded me. If I couldn't lift my arms, I could breathe. I could feel. I could move more of my body than any diagnosis could have ever sanely promised. Great grief filled me up, I seemed to breathe it, but what freed me was this: if my arms never worked again, never dressed myself, or combed my hair, if

I depended on others to do these things for the rest of my life, I no longer had to be, or even could be, who I once was. What I once was. I was broken. And new.

Nine weeks came with four long bolts screwed into my skull. I wanted the contraption off me. The whole time I hadn't showered: it had been impossible, encased in fiberglass and steel. And my hair shone with oil, dark and slick, glued to my scalp. After precautionary X-rays, the halo was approved for removal. I knew my neck muscles would be weak; doctors had warned they'd atrophy, after two months in which my head had been supported by bars.

An orthopedic surgeon came to my room with a tray of tools. I was in my wheelchair. He reclined it all the way back. Then he injected anesthesia into the skin near each bolt. With a torque wrench, he removed each one: there was no pain but I felt each one loosen, a weirdly abstract notion, as if it weren't really my head, my bone, that had been drilled into.

When all four were removed and put aside, the bars were disconnected from the vest and the halo lifted away. I lay still. The vest was unfastened. Finally, all of it was gone. Another collar was placed around my neck: I'd have to wear it until my neck regained its strength.

"Are you ready to raise up?" he asked. "Your neck will be very weak. Your head will feel like a huge weight. OK?"

I smiled. He was right. My head seemed enormous, impossibly heavy, and the muscles in my neck, so weak from months of disuse, screamed, burning. Days would pass before the pain would, when I'd begun to regain basic muscle tone.

He cleaned the holes in my head with gauze, mopping the caked gore that had built up over time. From each wound he tweezed long stray hairs and laid them aside.

Often I was bored, listless. The hallways would empty, and the floor go silent, save for the continuous weather of muffled machinery, respirators hissing unseen, monitors translating sickness into beeps. Patients withdrew into their rooms. Once I passed the room of a patient who had been injured a long time, years, while a respiratory therapist snaked a long, thin tube through the hole that had been cut into his trachea. The machine connected to the tube whirred and snuffled. A vacuum noise. The woman was drawing out the mucus his body couldn't expel. I could see it run, cloudy, thick, through the tube, away. His face was lunar with acne and he grimaced, clearly in pain.

When she was finished, she pulled a table back over to his chair. On the table was an easel, a magazine stand fixed with a mechanical arm to turn pages.

I left when I saw he was reading *Playboy*.

■

The gymnasium at night was always empty but the stereo was usually left on, filling up the space with music. While driving my wheelchair in long circuits around all the mats and between the exercise equipment, I'd listen, humming along. Through the windows I could see Atlanta's skyline, which stood on a high ridge above the surrounding land. Whole evenings I lost in those windows, while top forty played all around.

That night, the night I watched the phlegm be sucked from anonymous lungs, I went into the gymnasium; I could hear music. Lonely, sad for what I'd just seen, I was hoping someone might be there to talk to. I looked around but no one was there. I turned my head, scanning the room, and when I did, something gave way inside my neck. There was no pain in it. Not really. But it stopped me cold, right there in the gymnasium doorway, and though I had no reason to think it, I knew then that all the months in the halo, with my spine held immobile, had been for nothing. That I'd soon face the surgery we'd hoped to avoid. There was no real pain. Just an undeniable *wrongness*, a sense that something had shifted.

It scared me. I asked to go to bed early. I told no one.

When my parents were waiting for me in my room, in the middle of the week, I wasn't surprised. The day before, my spine had been X-rayed; I had hoped against all hope the results would be fine, though I knew my neck felt wrong, unstable.

"What are you doing here," I said, less like a question than they must have expected. I'd been downstairs in another patient's room, inspecting his new wheelchair, an awful purple.

"Yesterday we got a phone call," my mother began tentatively, looking to my father, whose skin seemed made of old ash. "There's something still wrong with your neck."

I had known it. But then I couldn't say anything, too scared, too miserable to consider it. A part of me was angry, too: angry that the halo hadn't worked and angry all that time had been for nothing. But it was eclipsed by the fear I felt, which had been seeded one week ago.

"You're going to have surgery tomorrow," my father said. "It's urgent."

"When?" I croaked. "Can't it wait a day or two? What time tomorrow?"

"Early. It has to be tomorrow. It has to be, Paul. This isn't something that can wait."

"We're going to be here," my mother said. "We'll be here the whole time. When you wake up, we'll be waiting. And everything will be all right."

If I had ever been so swamped by mortal sadness, I don't remember it. The surgery seemed a gross insult, a piling on, pain added to so much pain.

I smiled. Or tried to. Tried again. My parents did the same.

When they came for me, it was early. Not quite light. I'd slept well, after a while, after my parents had left for their hotel room. They'd see me in the morning, they promised. At first, in the raggedy fog of waking, nothing was wrong, nothing seemed amiss. Then there were my parents again, stepping in with coffee. We spoke a little while. Nurses soon came, administered a slight sedative to calm me. The last thing I remember is my mother's face.

chapter

FIVE

Up I swam through the floodwaters of morphine-deepened sleep, dreaming nothing, and opened my eyes. The ceiling like sky drifted. I was covered to my shoulders with a warm blanket. Everything seemed to glow. To be light like an incandescent bulb. My only thought was that I had not felt so good in months and nothing hurt and then I sank again. I wouldn't wake back up for twenty-four hours and when I did, it would be awful.

Nurses had come to turn me from my back to my left side. Beneath me was a folded sheet; I could be turned by pulling one side of the sheet against my body. One of them spoke.

"Time to turn, honey," she said. "This may hurt a little."

I could see my father, seated by the window, reading in its light. He began to stand up, as if he might offer his help. Then they turned me.

Pain cut through me, so severe I was amazed, stunned by the instant eradication of all the ease I had felt. The incision blazed. I had been opened up from my hairline to my shoulder blades and then closed with staples, so that the nape of my neck resembled a long, ghastly zipper.

Accustomed to pain, to great pain, even, I was, nonetheless, in no way able to ignore it, push it back. I screamed. Wept. They didn't stop. Could not. As much as the turn hurt, the nurses had to do this and I needed it, no matter the discomfort. When they left, I sobbed. My father came to my side, leaning in close. He was a young man still, tall and lean, with hangdog eyes, though I had no sense of that perspective. He was my father. He touched my shoulder, almost, his hand stopping in the air. The pain was beginning to fade to a wracking throb. My face was tacky with tears.

"Sometimes I think—" he said, his voice quavering and low. "Sometimes I think I haven't been a very good father to you."

He was tenderhearted and I knew this, but even more, he was prone to practical jokes, pretending one thing or another and never very well. I thought, at first, he was playing, mistaking the rawness of his grief, the largeness of it, for another dumb ruse. I began to say something, but stopped before any words came. His head had bowed like it was his neck that had been broken, incapable of holding up his face to mine. He shook with tears.

"Oh, Dad," I said, shocked, for a moment forgetting my neck. "Oh, no, don't say that. No, that's not true, you have been good."

He didn't say anything for a while, crying that way. I felt helpless in a new, almost larger way. Whatever had gone before, however sad or terrifying, I knew that this was worse. I knew that my injury had changed everything and everyone, forever.

"I've been reading the Bible," he said, when he could speak again, palming the tears off his face and from his inflamed eyes. "About Job. I want you to remember this verse."

He reached for the Bible he'd put aside when I screamed, thumbed through the pages.

"Job 23:10: *When He hath tried me, I shall come forth as gold.*"

I didn't say anything, though the meaning was clear.

"You're being tried, Paul. We all are. But when it's all over, you'll be like gold. Believe that. Believe that for me, OK?"

I had been raised in a church that was largely filled with the old. A province of the dying. Its long hallways smelled like time. Everything I learned, everything I was taught, was apocalyptic, was mortal. Still, I'd never learned this verse be-

fore. I would believe it, I said, and my father kissed my forehead, lightly, like something broken, about to break again.

After the atrophy of my neck muscles while wearing the
halo, and the painful period in which the muscles had to re-
strengthen, I hated how the surgery had cut through them.
I hated that I was forced to wear a collar again. At night,
the skin of my neck itched; the incision throbbed. Maybe,
just maybe, I hoped, this was the end of this particular pain.
Maybe, after miserable months, my neck would be whole
again, no longer the focus of so much discomfort.

What I learned after surgery, when my time at Shepherd seemed to have no discernible end, that I might stay
there forever, was that I was, all the time, being considered.
Measured. When I no longer made any real progress, I'd be
discharged, sent back to my home. The thought scared me. I
would watch the large marker board by the nursing station,
on which patients were moved from stage to stage. I feared
to see my name move from its initial column. I watched
other patients, some I knew, progress and then be marked
for discharge. In a few days, they'd be gone. At some point,
I would leave as well, leaving an environment in which no
one was particularly different, and entering my old world,
my old life. I'd be the changed thing, then.

Muscle spasms began to knot the muscles in my legs at night.
All night, sometimes. The muscles would violently contract,

and no medicine helped. Nurses would try at night to stretch them, to massage the muscles into stillness, but nothing worked. A nurse was once knocked to the floor while trying her best to help me, my leg resting atop her shoulder as she straightened it. Morning would come, slowly, and I would feel like a dishrag, wrung out by powerful hands. Doctors suggested it might always be this way: my damaged nervous system misfiring wildly into the night. Whenever someone said this, inside I shrank back from the thought. It was all I could do.

In the end, these long nights, when my legs seemed to be banded by iron, lasted two years, long past my hospitalization. There was no moment when I knew it was ending; only, a gradual subsiding, a storm of outraged nerves finally calming.

One evening in the middle of the week I was taken to a shopping mall with other patients. Accompanied by recreational therapists, we wandered about, a strange bunch of shoppers in wheelchairs, who couldn't breathe, whose urine hung in bags from their chairs or on their legs, in plain sight, who were embittered, depressed, even suicidal and maybe dying. We rode up in the mall elevators, whole groups at a time, while women with bags from Macy's clucked their impatient tongues behind us.

I loved to go out, to see some new place, and I didn't

much care that others watched us go by with mixtures of sadness, pity, and curiosity percolating in their faces. Old men would stop me, nosy and folksy all at once, their minds seeing the wiring of what we went about in.

"Young man," one might say. "Do you mind if I ask you something?"

At first, this was confusing, alarming, dreadful. I had no idea what I'd say if asked about any number of topics: what happened to me, would I get better, did I believe in Jesus.

"Sure, I don't mind," I'd reply, smiling big, smiling always.

"How many miles you think you can go in one of these?"

I really had no idea, then. I made up estimates. Five miles. Ten. Twenty. Whatever I thought would satisfy them, send us both our separate paths.

"There are two big car batteries in it, so it goes a long way."

"You don't mean it," he'd say, his voice a little distant, full of admiration. Something like this usually did the trick. I'd be blessed and notified I'd be appearing in his prayers and then we could part company, this bit performed.

And that night in the mall, eating ice cream fed to me by a therapist, I learned I'd soon be going home. When the cone was finished, the therapist hopped up, and his hand darted to the side of my wheelchair where a lever deactivated one of the chair's two motors. He'd disabled the left one and I looked back to him, shocked.

"Time you learned how," he said, hurrying away from me.

"How what?" I asked, annoyed.

"How to ask strangers for help," he called back, leaving me there. With one motor disengaged, the chair would only drive in long loops, difficult to control. With every turn, I could see my group trailing farther off. I was nervous, and angry with him. I tried to follow after them, circling, circling, watching all of them vanish. Then I ran over something. Someone.

"I am so sorry," I blurted, my face blushing instantly, my forehead dampening. It was a woman, tall and bookish-seeming, her eyes lost behind thick glasses. "They left me and they undid my motor and I can't catch up to them."

I was humiliated, blurting apologies to her. She put her hand to my shoulder, kindly, lightly.

"Oh, don't worry. I'm fine. Completely. Believe me, I'm used to a wheelchair running me over."

"Really?"

"My girlfriend has multiple sclerosis," she replied. "Used to be in remission but a few years ago it came back. She has a wheelchair like yours. It's older. We get around all right. Let me fix that."

She knew what to do and then wished me a good night. "No more circles," she said.

The prognosis for my recovery had never been exactly certain: at first, there was every reason to think I'd never move, never feel anything again. When that began to change, when my legs began to respond to therapy, and I could slowly extend them with light weights wrapped around each ankle, therapists wondered aloud, as we worked, if I might recover enough to walk again. Perhaps with a walker or crutches or other prosthetic devices, braces, splints, and dozens more, which would in time fill my closet and make of it a sad museum of hope. Perhaps, at least, I might be strong enough to push my own chair, and feed and bathe and dress my own body, however compromised. Perhaps any hundred degrees of recovery, of return, of resurrection, as though the life I lived were not exactly a life, but something else, in between, a limbo in which happiness was not quite possible, a hypothesis, a theory exhorted, but in half measures, in half consolations.

Therapists like Steve with his boundless empathy, and others I've forgotten, were stewards of my body and my hope, and between us passed the pain of never knowing when the end to that hope had undeniably come.

And so I knew that my time had come when nurses informed me I'd be taking my first trip back home for a weekend. I knew this visit was rehearsal for the day I was discharged, and for all the days which followed, for however long I lived with my family, dependent upon their care, and though no doctor would say it, that span of time might come to be forever.

■

I found out exactly as I feared I might. On the board beside the nursing station, my name had been moved into the last column, marked in red. I stared at it, deciding how I felt. Nearly five months of surgery, therapy, and daily pain had passed. Indignity after indignity and complete loss of privacy. Hundreds of strangers by then had seen my naked body, either in bed or in the hallway while I was rolled to one of the floor's several communal showers. It hardly mattered anymore.

But to return home? It had been a far off, undetermined day. Now it was no longer. Now I'd be sent home for a weekend visit, to live with my family again, though by everything that had happened we'd become impalpably estranged. I asked a nurse doing paperwork when my visit would take place.

"This weekend," she said. "Your parents will pick you up on Friday."

She returned to the work. I returned to my room, nervous, and said nothing to anyone.

When my parents came for me, I was waiting for them in my room, seated in a manual wheelchair, the kind that had to be pushed. Our van wasn't accessible: after being rolled inside the van on portable aluminum ramps, I rode the hundred miles home, reclined flat, staring up at the roof. At home, no ramp had been built yet; I couldn't go upstairs. I had to enter the house through the garage and into the downstairs den, connected to my old bedroom, and there spend the weekend, fed by my mother while everyone else, my dad, my three younger brothers, ate in the kitchen. There was no room for us all to be together; there was no other way.

The twins, Bo and Clay, were still babies, little more than a year old, and my middle brother, Chan, was only about eight: he said little all the while, nervous, hidden. My home felt unchanged. The walls downstairs were the same cheap wood paneling and the furniture was still mismatched; in the carpet was the same stain I'd made with yellow paint years before, up late with monster movies playing on our ancient television set.

All was the same, and, really, wasn't I also unchanged, in some essential manner, beyond the damage I'd brought to myself? *No*, I thought, *I'm not.*

Saturday night, late, after a day and a half of watching movies, eating meals cooked by my mother, visiting with my family, I lay in bed, sick, my stomach spiraling about itself. Whether it was the stress, the worry of the visit, or the change in diet from institutional blandness back to the old meals of greens and fried potatoes, corn bread and sweet tea, or a fear all this could go badly, I don't know. It was late, the room was dark except for the green luminescence of the digital clock beside my old bed, where my parents had lifted me into bed from my chair, and in my old bed my bowels had moved, staining all the sheets, my legs dirtied by each effort to move, to turn away.

I'd called for my mother and she had come, clearly tired. I thought that there was only one thing worse in all the world than this: not the asking for help, but its need.

"I've had an accident," I said.

"A bowel movement," she stated as much as she asked.

"Yes," I said, hating myself.

She was tired, moving through the fathoms of interrupted sleep, but she set to cleaning me, to changing the sheets. It took a while and we both were silent.

"Oh, Mother," I whispered near the last. "Am I a burden? I don't want to be a burden."

She snapped awake, stopping for the moment.

"A burden? No, how could you be? How could you be? Don't ever think that."

The next morning I left my home and family again, and on the road to Atlanta, reclined in the wheelchair, my sadness faded and a relief grew. I wanted to hate it, but I couldn't, not quite.

chapter

It was Halloween the day I was discharged. All around me, patients rushed about in makeshift costumes: spray cobwebbing and aluminum foil adorned their chairs. Balloons tied to them bopped in the trailing air. For the first time in almost six months, no nurses woke me early, sponged me clean before I wanted, and dressed me for the day. My parents were there, packing my things, gathering my clothes and taking cards I'd received down from the wall. I had little to bring home. It didn't take long to erase my presence. I felt sad to think another person would be admitted that day and assigned the same space that had been mine for so long. Sad for that unknown person's fate, for the rough months which awaited him, but sad, really, that I was leaving. No more complex than that.

I guess it was fitting to leave on Halloween. A day defined by masks. As trying, as painful, as my time there had been, it was an environment in which one could safely suffer and recover, away from the outside world. Now there were no illusions about the world to which I was returning, while all around me were patients pretending to be something else. Someone else. I said good-bye to a few nurses I knew, though no one who had been good to me seemed to be around. I looked into the gymnasium, which was half a party and half what it would always be, people struggling to reclaim their bodies, their lives.

Working at a machine designed to increase arm strength, Josh was absorbed in work. When I saw him, I felt my sadness, for a small moment, double. We had hardly been friends, just roommates separated by curtains, but he had been kind, a voice at night to laugh with, or complain. I went up to him, to say whatever good-bye I could. My eyes ached and I wanted now to leave, to go, to make this essential break with this place and the people in it.

"I'm leaving," I said, the best I could manage, tearing, my breath in raspy stitches.

"Hey, hey," he said, his right arm still strapped in. He couldn't move. "You're going to be fine. Don't worry. You're the only twelve-year-old I ever liked."

He clumsily smacked my knee with his weaker arm. I laughed and then I left, descending in the elevator with my parents, who helped me into the van. We pulled away.

It was terrifying to no longer be a patient. To no longer be in rehabilitation. In recovery. Unspoken, but quietly feared, was the assessment, by doctors, nurses, and therapists, that you had reached an endpoint in this process. That your rehabilitation had come to its expiration date. That nothing more could be done. What awaited was the rest of your life.

My parents had lifted me into the front passenger seat of the van. I could see the interstate spooling away as my father drove and we talked with my mother, seated in the rear, behind my wheelchair where it sat in the van's middle. Gradually, some of the gloom lifted from me: I hadn't sat in a car seat in months, since before my accident, and somehow it was gladdening to see the roads and cars and the underpasses slipping behind us. It was some little vestige of an old life, an activity which possessed no meaningful context, and yet I felt like each mile eased the worry just a bit. So much still loomed: where at home I'd sleep; when I'd return to school. The weight never left my mind and I wanted to know. I asked my mother.

"Where am I going to sleep? Not downstairs?"

"No, Chan has traded rooms with you," she said, leaning forward. "He'll be downstairs. He'll have your old room and the den. I know you hate that, but it's best."

"No, I know," I replied. It was best. The only bathroom I would have any access to was upstairs, along with the kitchen and my parents' bedroom. It was the only solution, though the bathroom was far too small for my wheelchair to even fit. My parents would have to lift me from my bed, naked, and carry me into the bathroom so that I could bathe, empty my bowels. Our house was fifty years old already, and small. I had understood, long before returning home, that it would be difficult for me to live there. I saw it in my mind and knew what would have to be done. To hear its confirmation was no surprise, yet it felt like one to a small degree.

"Chan isn't too crazy about it, but he understands," my father said.

"He agreed," called out my mother from the backseat of the van. We weren't far from home by then. I began to better recognize the low hills and the fields strangled by kudzu and the rare barn with SEE ROCK CITY emblazoned upon its roof.

"I don't want any sort of party," I said. "You remember that I asked that, don't you?"

"We do, don't worry," said my father, looking into the rearview mirror as he turned off the interstate. "We'll be home in a few minutes."

"I just don't want to deal with that. Not now. Not today."

Then my father pulled over on to the soft asphalt shoulder of the off-ramp and switched on the van's flashing emergency lights.

More lights, red and blue, began flashing behind us. A knock at the driver window. At first, only a blue field of officer uniform, then, lowering his face to ours, a state patrolman speaking.

"Is this the Guest family?" he asked, all gravity.

My father said that it was, that surely he hadn't been speeding.

"I'm here to escort you. Welcome back home, Paul."

He turned and went back to his cruiser, starting up the siren before pulling out, waving us to follow him. This might have been the last thing I had ever wanted, if I could have conceived of wanting this. I had no idea what it was, why a police escort blared through the streets of my small town. I wanted not to die but revert to some point in time when I was nonexistent.

My father was pleased by it all, driving slowly behind the car. He laughed, patting my shoulder vigorously, making turn after turn. People looked up from their yard work or their reading on their porches. Other cars pulled to the side of the road. Some waved, though they had no idea what was passing them. I hadn't said anything yet.

"Whose idea was this?" I asked miserably. "Who thought of this?"

Neither of my parents replied. I don't think the idea

was theirs, but they knew it would happen when we pulled off the interstate. Someone else, a friend of the family, a wildly misguided soul, someone with no gift of sense had devised it. All to welcome me back to my home and family and back to my life. I felt murderous, embarrassed, ready only to vanish.

When we turned at last into our driveway I could see our house. The sloping front lawn with a wild dogwood in its center and the backyard, fenced in, shadowed by the limbs of a large pecan tree. A ramp had been built, long and turning at right angles, rising until it reached our porch. A cement path led through the lawn, uphill to the ramp. All this was new. I'd enter and exit our home this way. Taught well the expense of everything my injury could ever touch, spilling ever outward, I knew it must have cost thousands, and my heart slumped in my chest. Some nights after my accident I would dream of sepia-tinted mushroom clouds. Seen in the old newsreels shown to us in school, to show what the end really would look like. I woke from those dreams startled, in a contentious sweat, *no no no*. Sitting there, imagining storms of fissure sprout around our house like weeds, I felt my heart slump in my chest. If I could be transparent, unseen, then I would not feel so bad.

People began streaming from the house and from inside the garage. They held signs above their heads and were applauding. People I knew from church, adults and their children, and relatives, cousins, uncles, aunts, grandparents,

and friends from school I had not seen since before my accident, some close to me and some not. Some that had been
at my accident. Adam. Jody wasn't there and wouldn't be
in the future: I saw her once more, though she didn't see
me, years later, shortly before she died of cancer. Neighbors. Friends of family, who had tirelessly raised money and
babysat and cooked, the sorts of things small communities
are programmed to do when there is awful news. When
there is a death.

Here I was, their tragic occasion, their almost death.
They clapped in the growing dusk while my parents lifted
me from the car seat and into the rented electric wheelchair. They shook their glittered signs at me, saying *notice*.
Shouting *praise Jesus* and *amen* and weeping where they
stood in the grass and I drove through them, nodding
stiffly, making eye contact with no one, up the new ramp
while everyone clapped all over again, as if there had been
worry over the successful navigation of it all, clapping and
clapping and clapping like a congregation of fools and for
the first time since breaking my neck, I thought, *I want
to die.*

chapter

SEVEN

I rode the short bus, awful slang for a bus intended for
children with special needs. Every morning, just past seven,
the short bus lurched to a wheezing halt in the street, a
frenetic suburban artery. Cars waited in long chains on either side as I was raised from the ground by a screaming
hydraulic lift. When I had been belted in and my chair
strapped by the driver, she rammed forward again, jolting
all her passengers to the bone. I hated it. Hated the every-
day exposure to the plain impatience of all the drivers who
waited, sometimes querulously honking their horns. Hated
the ensuing jostle, the careless velocity through every pot-
hole and over each speed bump which had the temerity to

appear in our path. And, though I was ashamed, a part of me hated the other passengers, who were blameless. Guilty only of their parents' poverty, or the faulty replication of DNA, they greeted me with loud hellos, or wordless recognition, waving, clapping silently, laughing, turning to me to chat when the short bus began again. One girl, her voice all twang, who lived on a hill above a Church of God of Divine Revelation, always wore the same shirt. She always asked me the same question.

"Do you know who Ricky Van Shelton is?" she cooed. I didn't. Her shirt showed me: he was mostly cowboy hat and serviceable pout, brooding with his guitar. A country singer, a knockoff of better, more authentic artists, but to her he was Elvis. Elvis reborn, I guess.

"I've never heard of him," I said, trying to be honest. She suggested I listen to him sometime. "I might do that. Thank you."

At first, this satisfied her, but only for a while. Soon, Ricky Van Shelton hardly mattered. And Elvis was a footnote. Older than me by a few years, she would sit in the rear row, to my left, and flutter until we reached school a few minutes away. I don't know what was wrong with her, or what had happened to her, if she had been born impaired or, like me, in some way, injured, frozen in time. She was breathless, already sexual, though she was unaware. I stared ahead or at the roof of the short bus while we bounced about and she glowed.

"Do you have a girlfriend?" she began to ask me every morning. At first, uncomfortable, I said no, which again was the truth.

"I would be your girlfriend," she said, so plainly that it hurt. Her eyes were large and dark and her hair a knotty, untended brown. "If you wanted me to be your girlfriend."

That word was fraught for her. *Girlfriend*. However much she understood of herself, she knew that there could be more. She knew desire.

Finally, after weeks of her eyes, her sad entreaties, I began to tell her that I did have a girlfriend, one who was very sweet. The same grief always took her face and changed it, and when I lied to her I longed for what I said to be true.

"That's OK," she would say, turning to the windows. "I'd still be your girlfriend, if you wanted me someday."

I had not wanted to return to school two days after my discharge from Shepherd, but I did. Two weeks, I'd asked for. Time enough to return home and make sense of living with my family again. Time enough to prepare myself for a new school, junior high, with new teachers and new students. It loomed large in my mind. But my parents insisted, and had already made plans for my enrollment. I didn't struggle with it. There were no arguments. Despite my desire for two weeks' respite, I knew it was the best thing I could do. November had come already. The air outside had begun to chill and become faintly brittle at night. The school year would soon be half over. Too late to salvage. I'd lose time, be held back, and that loss would be greater than the two weeks I wanted.

The junior high was old, built on a hill. Two stories but no elevator. Between classes, in rain, in sleet, I had to rush in a circuit around the campus, up a road, and back into the building. For two years I did this every day.

The school system provided a paraprofessional to write for and otherwise assist me: to help me at lunch and empty the catheter bag I wore around my calf, inside my jeans, when it filled up with urine. Her name was Louise. She was funny, outgoing, and had a gift for knowing when I needed her help and when to be transparent, to hang back, without inserting herself into my new life. It was only some years later that I realized how crucial that was, how lucky I was to work with someone like her.

I had harbored amorphous worries about my return to school. Beyond the early hormonal waves of fear which swamp every adolescent, when fitting in is everything, I fretted over what it would be like to enter class that first day, to be regarded by so many strange faces, how it would feel to join an already defined group. A class. A school. More than anything, I wanted to be invisible.

Those fears, multiplying in my blood, viral in their growth, were quashed by the teacher of my first class. I sat there before class began, before the haranguing clatter of bells in the hallway, while students who I didn't know filed into class, falling into their desks like surrender. When the hallways were empty, of students and noise, but before class began, she came to me, kneeling to make eye-level contact, usually a gesture I hate because it changes nothing that is different between us, and quietly said, "It's good that you're back and I'm glad you're in my class."

That was it. Nothing unctuous. Nothing grabby or glad-handed or intended to inspire me or notify me that I was an inspiration.

And it was true: it was good to be back and I was glad to be in class.

Ronnie began to ride the short bus not long after I did. He was lean, with long arms and splayed fingers. His hair, dark and slick, drew back from his forehead as if in retreat. His face narrowed to a point like a wedge and was scab-wet all over, malignant with acne. He wore heavy denim and his long-sleeved shirts were always stained. He never spoke. Not a word. I'm not sure he could speak and no one ever explained him to us, except to announce his name like a warning.

He lived in a trailer with adults I never assumed were his parents. Stooped and leathery, they rarely appeared, except to stand balefully beside the mailbox, smoking thoughtfully while the bus shuddered to a stop and the doors slid open for Ronnie. When the driver had seated him, they went back inside their home, having said nothing.

When the short bus started up again, Ronnie would rock back and forth where he sat alone. He made noises. Little whimpers. Snuffles at first that might have been troubled sleep. None of us spoke while he rode with us, watching him lurch.

Once, when the driver had stepped off the short bus and no one's eyes were on him but ours, Ronnie leaped up from his seat and moved lithely towards the back of the bus, where I sat. An obese girl, who was mute and had difficulty walking, sat across the way. He took her head in his arms, locked one around her throat, and was yanked away by the driver. The girl, weeping wildly, coughed and mewled and thrashed at the air.

He would take his fingers in his mouth, two or three at a time, and bite down on them, still rocking, until they bled from his mouth and down his chin and onto his shirt.

Still rocking.

A squeal now like the rasp of a saw through wood.

Still rocking.

And then, through all the short bus, through all its confined space, the stink of his shit would go, while he smiled and bled.

Every day for a year this happened.

We all tried not to breathe. To deny that air.

Every day on the short bus from which none of us could escape.

chapter

When school was over, the short bus would lower my chair
by hydraulic lift into the street. At our front door, my mother
waited for me to come up the long ramp to the porch and
let me inside, though there was little room to freely move
about. The hallway to my bedroom was so narrow both sides
of my wheelchair dug long trenches into the sheetrock. So
that I could enter and exit my bedroom the frame around
the doorway had to be removed. Inside, there was a hospital
bed with rails pushed up against a wall. I had a small desk,
high enough for me to roll under, and an old typewriter. To
the right, the other wall. If I turned around in the room, I

had to be careful of my toes: they would hit the bed or the desk or the wall.

And there was less room when Chan began to sleep on a small mattress on the floor beside my bed. Every night for almost a year we slept this way. The room had been his. It had always been his. Downstairs, where the den and my old bedroom were dug into the earth and were always dark and cool, he had never been comfortable. He was a child, eight years old, quiet and shy. One night, soon after my return, he wanted to watch a late-night movie with me. He never left.

At home, my mornings began, even earlier than they had at Shepherd, with exercise while I was still in bed. First, my mother stretched my legs as best she could, straightening them, rocking my hips from one side to the other. Then she helped me raise my knees and immobilize my feet: I lifted my bottom from the mattress by flexing my quadriceps. It was hard work for me, and harder for her, a small, compact woman. After thirty minutes she dressed me and because the bathroom in the hallway beside my bedroom was too small, I brushed my teeth in the kitchen sink and washed my hair in a plastic basin on the kitchen table with thick towels wrapped around my neck and in my lap to catch all the spillage. It was no good, but it was the best way we had.

■

Across from the cramped bathroom I couldn't enter, on the wall hung a rustic frame, and in that frame was a painting of an old tree, its limbs arthritic and dense with foliage, standing a crooked guard beside a dirt road which rutted off into a dark distance. Carved into the tree's scarred bark were my parents' initials: JG & PG. James and Paula. When I was a boy, awake before everyone, I would sometimes stand on the tips of my toes to better consider it. Their names, right there, set into both the wood and the paint, fascinated me. Warm with the breath of a heating grate, I could not be hurried from them.

The town they grew up in is dead now. Dead, though it's caught between the last gasp and whatever follows after it. Or doesn't.

Along its main boulevard, used car lots loiter beneath ragged banners. Adult bookstores wait behind mandated facades, identified by their facelessness. Pawnshop windows dump neon light into the sullen day. Check-cashing services promise not to take your car.

But on the corner was an ice cream shop, a greasy spoon, the sort of place in which all things were sallow chrome and smelled like grease, grease forever, and onions and beef cooked in common on a grill, right there in front of you, by some kid who, as the story goes, is going to get out of here, somehow, some way, or an old woman with her silvering hair bound up in a net, with her arms like hams and her face not much different and her cough rattling around inside of her like a baby's toy.

When I was a boy, I would go with my father to vacuum his car. Loose coins in the blue hoses clattered and I loved that noise. A fastidious hail. Perched on a block while he worked, I waited for him to be done, to take my hand and lead me across the street to the ice cream shop, which seemed ancient to me, a relic from outside everything I knew and was.

We ordered swirled soft-serve vanilla, injected into sugar cones, and sat atop stools with swiveling seats at the grimy bar. The hiss of grease sang out.

Outside, in the quiet street, a lone car might trundle past, slowing, almost as if the driver were lost, searching about for crumbling landmarks, a sign which pointed away.

Another image, this time a photo of my parents, senior prom, my father in rented tuxedo with wing-wide lapels, and my mother, seated, her hair longer than I have ever seen it, a dark wash down her back. Fake backdrop behind them, they're beautiful. Untouched. Burdened by nothing.

When I was seven, I begged for cowboy boots until my mother relented, and then I slept in them and would not stop, though I woke every morning with feet soaked in sweat and my body so hot I felt ill. Too expensive to subject to the playground minefield, the boots stayed behind when I left home, old sneakers on my feet. I loved the boots, and had wanted them after months of comic book back cover advertisements. In them, O. J. Simpson struck an unbothered, post-disco pose, and whatever he said, whatever pablum devised by copywriters, meant nothing to me, except that these boots, all leather heavy, were what I wanted more than anything in that world.

Never very good at most sports, not baseball, slow enough that I vanished into daydream and caught nothing, and not basketball, which proved physically foreign in a way I could never master, every shot comically errant, I could, however, play soccer. The local recreation league games were held on autumn Saturday mornings, when dew was still on the grass and the sun was low in the sky. I tended to slip into the stiff cleats, having left the laces loose, and when I struck the ball one cleat would sail across the field like an oblong bird, shot mid-flight.

When my first season ended, and there was no tournament future for us, we were invited to a party at the coach's house. He lived in a neighborhood that rolled up and down, every lawn and driveway a minor slope. After food, after blistered hot dogs and canned pork beans served cold to us on paper plates, we went down into the garage to find ways to pass the time because, really, we hardly knew each other,

appearing once a week to run around in half-coherent fash-
ion and be yelled at by a stranger, some man who acted
as though he had power over us, and when the inevitable
realization came that we were children, and not him, not
him at all, the yelling faded out and the game ended soon
enough, just as the day grew warm.

His son had a skateboard and began surfing down the
driveway. A few times before others joined in, rolling to
a stop in the gravel, jumping off, tumbling, laughing and
running back up the driveway to start it all over again. I
watched, laughing, hooting for those who kicked the board's
nose up and ground its tail into the asphalt, stopping.

I knew this was nothing I was any good at. Boys waved
to me from the bottom of the hill while one of them ran
back up the hill with the skateboard held out in his arms.

Come on! One time! Chicken!

I took it from the boy and considered what to do. I
wanted to do it because I loved velocity and plain motion.
I loved to watch the movement of the world: cars blurring
past our home in hot gusts of wind and boats splitting the
waters of a river and the shifting procession of clouds in the
summer sky. I felt called to it, always.

I lay down on the board and pushed off from the launch
of the garage, rolling low to the ground, faster than I had
expected. All the boys yelped: none of them had expected
this.

My face was inches from the asphalt and my arms hugged the skateboard to my chest. There was now the question of stopping and I had no answer for it.

Later, when the party had ended and our dispersal had begun, I climbed into my mother's waiting station wagon. It was dark, night fallen fully down in the crisp air. I entered through the front seat, the car's dome light igniting as I climbed over the front seat and into the back. I was tired, bleary, already tugged at by sleep as I tumbled into the back, propping my boots on the passenger side's headrest. As she turned to back up, her eyes fell on the ravaged toes of my boots, burned through when I had dragged them like anchors down the driveway.

The car stopped and she roughly turned the boots to her face.

"What did you do to these?" she demanded, looking down to where I had fallen behind her seat. "Take them off, give them to me, let me see them now."

I shucked them off meekly, terrified and sad: I had not realized what had happened to the boots, how they had been ruined. I'd had no idea.

Screaming, she threw one. It thudded against the back window. And then the other came down, missing me by inches.

I gathered it up in my arms and cowered on the floorboard, holding it like a trophy of my own foolishness. We drove home.

That night now seems like a precursor to the morning of my injury, when I did not know enough to avoid damage, when I wanted so badly for my body to be other than it was, but not, if I could have known, what it would become, when nothing could protect me from myself, not even my parents.

chapter

Junior high dances were loud pageants of melancholia, held in the school cafeteria, darkened, festooned with glittering tinsel, loud with heavy metal, a prelude to the suffocating sway of pop ballads. I went alone but tried to speak to friends, yelling above the decibels. It felt like torture, like something inside me with deep roots was slowly being pulled out.

The air was dense with noise and hot: the ecosystem of the young. From a corner, I watched couples pair off, draw close when the ballads played. Teachers threaded through the crowd with flashlights, clicking them on when someone danced too close to their partner, when kissing began. Weak bursts of light winked through every song.

I longed to join them. To participate in the communal swoon. But in another body. Not the one I had. I refused the half-measure of attempting to dance in my chair.

Because it would be no more than that: an attempt.

There were times I could have. When the Trundle sisters, already matronly, faced me on both sides, clumsily writhing, suggesting sensuality, I shook my head, shouted them away, hating them for even trying to involve me. We were strangers and we always would be.

A girl who had a crush on me, a sweet, attentive soul who always spoke in the halls, who passed me handwritten notes declaring her feelings, once came to me in the dark while everyone else pressed their bodies together, and knelt beside me. She spoke into my ear.

"Would you dance with me?"

I didn't say a word. I was unable. All the breath inside my lungs stopped. She put her warm arm around the back of my neck and touched her forehead to mine.

For as long as that song lasted, she touched me that way. Not moving. Quiet. Her arm around me. As the song ended, I thought to kiss her forehead.

To press my lips to her skin like an apology.

But I did nothing and when the music began again she stood up, smiling sadly, and walked away, back into the crowd, where she vanished, though I tried to see her.

And then, it was over: the dance, the night, and soon enough, junior high, where I learned that longing is the body's true lesson.

The hair of Bob Burnes recalled the weirdly inviolable, spray-shellacked dome of a television evangelist. He had been the principal of my elementary school at the time I broke my neck, a devastated, weeping visitor in the first days following my injury. Three years later, at the start of high school, he would be my principal again. That summer, in the days before classes began, I thought of what it would be like to see him, a reminder of my past, and felt indefinably blank.

No part of my injury had been his fault, though it happened at the home of one of his teachers. I'd known him in the way any child feels he knows a teacher, or visible administrator, which is to say that when I saw him in the hallways of my elementary school I thought, *He knows me but no one else. I am special. I will be remembered.*

And I would be, of course.

A few weeks before the start of the school year, I visited the new campus to inspect it for any issues with accessibility. I roamed empty halls, more interested in battered lockers and old textbooks stacked in precarious columns. Rounding the blind corner of an enormous trophy case, filled with fading jerseys and retired numbers, trophies, plaques, and photographs from other decades, I almost ran over him. We had both been distracted but we stopped, exhaling before we spoke.

"Isn't it good to find you here," Bob Burnes said. He seemed to be speaking to himself, repeating something to himself that was, in fact, gladdening. He touched my shoulder, lightly, afraid I might suffer from any touch. "I'm glad to see you."

"It's been a while," I said. "Are you liking it here?"

He had just been promoted to the high school. He sat down on a wooden bench, looking down the long, featureless hallway, turning something over in his thoughts.

"Promise me one thing, Paul," he said, his voice still far away. "In four years, when you graduate . . ."

He trailed off, weighing the thing he wanted to say. I waited for him, though a dread began to build inside of me. I didn't say anything.

"When you graduate, I want to see you walk across that stage," he said, facing me now, very much present, his eyes wet and bright. "Can you promise me that?"

I said the only thing I could. I promised to walk across my graduation stage.

By any reckoning, it was an awful thing to ask, as though all that had held me back in the three years since breaking my neck was a cringe-inducing request in a high school hallway. As if I had been waiting around for the right challenge, as if a high school graduation ceremony were the glory of my youth and I should cross it in full stride.

When I promised him I'd walk again, it was a promise I knew I'd never be able to keep. Enough time had passed for me to know, for me to feel in my body, that I'd come to the ends of any real physical improvement: no more strength was going to return to any part of my body, at least nothing that would be of practical use.

No morning would come when I'd wake and find my arms restored from the atrophy that had already taken place. My legs wouldn't bear me up like a miracle.

I had reached the end of the body's capacity to heal itself. There was no more. Though this was something too painful for loved ones to hear, who kept a vigil in their hearts for me, I had made my peace with it. This was my body and this was my life.

A new school brought a nearly maddening chain of new assistants. The night before the first day of classes Sharon called our home to see if she could come by for a visit, to meet before the next day's first bell. When she arrived, my mother invited her into our living room. She sat primly, clutching a purse, absently touching her hair like she was nervous, on edge. My mother asked her where she was from.

My mother prided herself on detecting any hint of a person's birth.

"I'm from Scranton," Sharon said. "Pennsylvania. Not far from Philadelphia."

"It's cold there," my mother offered.

"That's why I like it here," she replied. "Nice warm weather. We were ready for a change. Me and my husband."

It was the sort of talk I hated. Idle and weightless, going nowhere. I imagined it five days a week, and my eyes wanted to cross. I stared out the window at the lawn, which was withered in the summer heat, the last of it, before autumn's onset. After a while, I realized I was being discussed.

"Paul wears a leg bag," my mother said. "Are you familiar with what one is?"

Sharon shook her head stiffly. Her dark beehive of hair floated above her like a hint of bad weather. My mother reached over to me, raising the left leg of my jeans to expose the plastic bag, half filled, strapped around my calf, and the tube with a valve hanging down.

"You might have to empty this sometimes," she said breezily. "If it gets full. With urine. His urine."

She nodded blankly, watching my mother.

"Don't worry, it's easy," my mother said, standing up. "Let me show you."

She walked away. Sharon, who appeared to be shrinking with every minute, smiled approximately. I imagined her like a character in a comic book, with a thought balloon rising up from her mind, except there was nothing in the balloon. Nothing.

When my mother returned, she was holding a Mason jar. She knelt on the floor beside me and sat the glass jar on the carpet by my left foot.

"This is what we empty Paul's urine into. All you do," she said, "is take the tube and it has this plastic snap—"

Urine puddled on the dark navy carpet. She had opened the valve accidentally.

"Oh, shit," my mother said brightly. "I wasn't being careful. No big deal. I'll just get a washrag and scrub this right up. That just happens sometimes."

The woman looked over at me, miserably. I felt a little sorry for her. Soon, the spill was cleaned up and the jar returned to the bathroom. We resumed our meeting.

"I should be going, I suppose," the woman said.

"Oh, don't rush off," my mother said, patting my knee. "Would you like some sweet tea?"

"No, thank you very much," she said. "I do have two questions. Well, one is more of a statement and the other is a question."

"OK," I said, listening sickly.

"The first thing I should tell you is that I can't spell. I can't. You will really have to help me on that."

"I imagine we'll work that out," I suggested, spotting my mother in the corner of my eye. She wouldn't look back, a forced smile on her face.

"And my question," Sharon said, her face very serious now. I tried to think of what she wanted to know, ran my mind through the usual catalog of queries: *What happened to me? Had I been born this way? Did I have a personal relationship with the Lord?*

"Go on," I said, bracing myself for whatever she wanted to ask.

"Will there be someplace where I can keep my purse?"

I had the same cheery rictus as my mother and the thought balloon which rose from my head like pale smoke read, *Fuck fuck fuck fuck fuck.*

chapter

E-V-E-R-Y L-E-T-T-E-R O-F E-V-E-R-Y W-O-R-D. N-O
M-A-T-T-E-R H-O-W S-I-M-P-L-E, N-O M-A-T-T-E-R
H-O-W S-E-E-M-I-N-G-L-Y O-B-V-I-O-U-S.

In class, Sharon's job was, ostensibly, to take notes while
a teacher lectured or write my answers on class work or tests.
Instead, I whispered in her ear every letter of every word of
every line of notes I needed for every class, while attempting to disturb no one else: my classmates, whose pens and
pencils sped across the pages, and my teachers, who listened
to the class-long mutter I made in her ear with growing frustration.

■

A biology teacher, grim and humorless, watched Sharon flail every day with increasing disdain. Before class one day, he came to where we sat. He fixed her in his flat gaze.

"I can give you my lecture notes," he offered her, acidly. "It might improve the, ah, *situation*."

That word was drawn from his mouth like a serrated blade, meant to cut, and he had expected it would. I could see it. He waited for her to flinch.

"Oh, no, goodness no, thank you," she said. Her round face beamed.

He looked to me, a brief softness in the long shape of his face before it hardened for her. He began recording his lectures at night, passing me cassette tapes when class ended and she had already left the classroom. Sometimes there were hand-drawn diagrams of cellular structures, complicated explications of processes, and obsessive, enthralling passages on etymology. Language itself was a living thing and all its secrets were also its possibilities. I think my first training as a writer, as a poet, began then, though I had no idea of this at the time. Even as Sharon labored beneath the shroud of language, I grew to love what it could reveal.

Sharon's hand would shake, scrawling out mistake upon mistake, while I hissed, *no no no* and finally *yes*. I consigned myself to watching written rubble pile up on the page.

She laughed nervously, rubbing the pencil's eraser entirely away until its metal end tore through, making a long, pulpy accordion in the page. She would reach for another sheet, solemnly, and start over. By the end of each class, a fraction of that day's lesson had been successfully taken down. When the bell rang, Sharon would hide for a few moments in the teachers' lounge, where her purse was stowed in an open cubbyhole.

I followed her there once, entering the offices by another door, and from a distance watched her seated beside a humming soda vending machine, her eyes locked on the purse, as though it were a hatchling that might be blown from the nest.

I felt guilty when, after two months, I requested that we no longer work together. And I felt guilty when, the following summer, a postcard arrived from Reading, Pennsylvania.

The writing on the back of the card appeared to have been written by someone else, with none of Sharon's blocky, all-caps lettering. The message read:

> *Hi Paul! I think of you often. Hope you are well. We have come to back to PA and are happy. But cold! You may write (if you wish) to this address.*

I felt no guilt when I ignored the card, letting it become buried by books and papers, and, most of all, by time. I couldn't bear the thought of contact with her. A residual degree of frustration and anger lingered in me like a venom.

Now, that is gone, replaced with clarifying irony: she must have been dyslexic, or beset by some other cognitive disorder, none of which I am in any way qualified to diagnose. But it makes a kind of sense, or it helps me to think more kindly of her and feel, in all my fallibilities, all my incapacities, a long, latent, wounded empathy.

Days after Sharon's replacement began working with me, I began to wonder if I had been rash, if, maybe, by the school year's end, if I had not murdered Sharon, things might have improved. If I might have somehow been able to train her in the inscrutable mysteries of the alphabet. If all the stars and all the planets, everything strewn about the cosmos like burning litter, might have lined up like glowing cherries in a Las Vegas slot machine, hitting jackpot, with all the letters and then all the words tumbling forth in a slurry of golden sentences. I wondered this.

Hiding from her replacement in the stacks of the school's modest library, pretending to be interested in biographies of Oliver North and Bob Dole, I wondered this.

Jennifer, or Jen as she wanted me to call her, had appeared with a mug of coffee in her hands, a voice that tittered and trilled and then softened to instant sobriety, her heart larded with grief. For me, for you, for the children she someday intended to bring forth into the world.

She could spell, quickly, perfectly, and for a short moment I felt like maybe this would be better. This would work.

But when Jennifer asked me what had happened to me, and listened with perfect gravity to my story, her eyes fattened with tears. She touched my forearm.

"You have been through so much," she whispered. "So, so very much."

"It, ah, hasn't been so bad," I said. In situations like this, when a stranger's grief appears ready to ignite, I tried to tamp down their sense of my suffering.

"You are so wise," Jennifer said, her hand still nestled on my arm. I pulled it from her touch, onto my lap, but she didn't notice. "Let me help you."

Gingerly, she took my arm in her hands, returning it to my wheelchair's armrest. Anger spiked inside me. I pulled away once more. We were in the library, during a study period. Students moved about in bored circles.

"I'm going to look up some books," I said, more forceful than necessary. Her eyes blinked. "You stay here."

"Yes, of course, Paul," she said, her voice wounded. "You take your time. I'll be right here."

■

As much as I had learned to inhabit my body, with all its changes and difficulties and outright agonies, I had been forced to try to respond to strangers who didn't see me in my broken state, in pain, struggling, so much as they saw their son or daughter. As they saw themselves. For all the gentle curiosity, the questions about which batteries my wheelchair used, or how I used the bathroom, people couldn't help their fascination with ruin. With their future selves. The downward arc of dotage. In me, they could see a rehearsal of the flesh, how it might all end.

I could say nothing to her that wasn't suffused with heroic stoicism: in her eyes, I was a vessel for suffering. Or courage. Maybe pluckiness. Maybe all of the tired tropes which had been pinned to my life like a badge. There was nothing I hated more fervently than playing that imaginary role. A consolation to others but not to me.

And, yet, I understood it. I felt it. The urgency of grief, even when utterly misguided, when knotted in self-interest.

That spring the radio stations in town, the little ones which seemed to warble from a great distance, broadcasting thundering, disembodied Sunday sermons, began advertising an upcoming appearance by Joni Eareckson Tada. The teenager whose book I skimmed through the night before my injury was now grown, married, in charge of a large foundation and host of a syndicated radio show. My mother requested free tickets for us both, though I had no desire to go, to participate in or be defined by disability, whether it was mine or that of someone else. My mother replied: *You're going anyway.*

I wanted no part of going and wanted nothing from her story. I knew enough of my own injury to understand how changed I was and how set apart.

The venue's stage was flanked on both sides by paintings Tada had completed by gripping a brush in her teeth. A lamb, a lion, a glade exploding with summer. We waited while the room continued to fill up and metal parts clanked and unseen bodies groaned and the metallic hiss of respirators went up into the air.

After a short while, a woman wheeled Tada up a ramp beside the stage and to its center where the light fell down on her. Nearly forty, she was no longer a wounded girl in a book. More than ever, I wanted to leave.

Tada was dressed in bland clothes; her brown hair was pulled back. Everyone clapped and flash bulbs began to pop throughout the crowd. Tada waited for the applause to boil off before she spoke, greeting us. Her voice was warm and practiced, every syllable liquid. Then she began to sing. There was no music. Only her voice.

Her arms swept slowly over us all. Her wrists were supported by splints. Around me, eyes began to shine with tears.

When the moment had passed, and her song was over,

she spoke a short while. God allowed to happen what he hated, she said, so that what he loved might be accomplished.

I wanted to leave, to run from the room and everything so simple and palliative, but I couldn't.

Tada sang a lilting benediction before thanking us all and turning to sign books at a table. I refused to go up, to meet her, and moved to the dimly lit back of the room where I could watch the broken parade. My mother never quite joined the line, talking instead to the woman who had pushed Tada onto the stage.

When my mother waved me forward, she introduced me to the woman, a friend of Tada and co-host of the daily radio show syndicated around the world. The woman smiled sweetly and walked over to Tada, whispering in her ear, and pointing to me. Tada smiled and waved to me from where she sat signing her books. I smiled back but felt false, repulsed: this was not what I ever wanted to be, not for anyone, an example, a symbol.

At school, I continued to work with Jenny, though I spent much of it avoiding her. In the quiet spaces of the day, she hinted at the sadness of her marriage. I stared off, into whatever distance was available, while she morosely leaked. All I wanted was to complete my work with minimal disruption.

If I said nothing in reply to her, she returned to writing, or doodling, making small hash marks on the page, like she had been taught by experience to be ignored.

On the year's final day, while students darted every-where, manic to be done, we sat in the hallway chatting. Weeks ago she had informed me she wouldn't be back to work with me again and I had almost swooned with relief, though I feigned a dim regret.

"I want to tell you something," she said while looking downward. "I said there were things I needed to better focus on in my life."

"Yeah," I agreed. "You said that."

"That's not exactly true," she almost choked out. "This is hard for me to say. Very hard. Please don't think I'm strange. I couldn't stand that."

I didn't say anything. She went on.

"I— I've— The best way to put it is—" She broke off. "I have developed feelings for you. Serious feelings."

I still said nothing. My mind had lit out for a sane place in the world.

"*Emotions*," she said. She imagined, I think, that her voice in that crucial moment was italicized. I just blinked. She stumbled on.

"I'm seeing my pastor." She blushed. "I mean, he's guid-ing me. I told him a few weeks ago. He told me I had to quit. Please don't be angry with me."

She was close to sobbing now. She vibrated pitifully.

"I'm—uh—not," I said. "Not angry."

"I'm so happy," she cooed. "I'm so happy—"

"I'm leaving," I interrupted, already in motion. "I have to go. Good-bye."

At the sidewalk's far end, behind the long snout of a cargo van, I hid, even though the June sun stabbed and I soon felt ill in the heat. Students pulled away from the school in their shitty cars, stereos pounding the air, tires smoking expertly as they accelerated, while all around me an emptiness grew.

I think now of my first kiss. Not the ordinal kiss of childhood, planted on my lips like a solemn playground dare. No, I was fifteen, a high school freshman, on the yearbook staff, working with a partner, a girl named Kelly, after school in the yearbook room, a small closet that was mostly drawers and shelves stocked with layout pages and red wax pencils. I didn't care for it, and when the year was done, I wouldn't stay. Nearing a deadline, we were forced to stay late, to finish our assigned pages. All the school was emptied out and no one cared that we listened to a radio. That we accomplished mostly nothing.

She was tall, red-haired, denim-draped, always. I hardly knew her, except that she was kind to me, watchful. She was the type of girl to come to school with a bruised eye, the mottled flesh seemingly so ordinary, so daily, she took little effort to conceal it. It would come and go, a chronic mark.

I didn't notice when she drew close, not until I felt on my face the heat of her neck. I turned to face her, dropping the mouth stick I type and turn pages with.

You, she said. And nothing more. She touched my face with her hand, black polish on her nails chipped away in places, white-pink beneath. There was the tang of bad cigarettes.

She kissed me, sweet and chaste, rubbing the back of my neck. I returned her kiss, half in terror, half in confusion. Then it was time for us to leave.

I watched her climb into an old lime Ford Torino. Her boyfriend peered into the distance, unaware she had opened the door, sat down, until she touched his face and they began to sign, making words with their hands because he was deaf.

The sky was huge, almost spring, surrendering to the night. They kissed lightly and he eased from the curb. Kelly turned to look out the passenger side window. She saw me, a long and lengthening distance away, and mouthed what I thought was a silent *no*. Her hands were still.

■

The first poem I ever wrote came to me like an accident of the mind. A blip, noise that had no apparent cause. Bored in class, watching classmates perform group activities near the end of the school year, when teachers were as desperate for escape as we were, I was thinking of nothing particularly literary, watching the sky and the visible world happen outside the window, when I began to hear in my head the rhythms of language, the propulsive patterns of a poem, and though I had no idea why, it was suddenly imperative that I write it down. Typewriters still populated the world in relative numbers back then, and it was easy to find one in the library, and blank paper beside it, ready to be covered. I began typing with my mouth stick what I heard, as well as I could render it, and when I finished it, a part of my brain had lit up, or switched on. Sitting there, that's how I explained the sensation to myself as it galvanized me. There was no doubt, none, that I had stumbled on to something essential about myself, who I was and who I might become, and all around me the future seemed to crackle like a storm.

This is what I'm supposed to do, I thought. After that moment, I never doubted it.

On an early summer evening beneath a dusk-marbled sky I broke a promise I never believed I could keep: I did not walk across my graduation stage, did not take diploma in hand, in stride, and walk off into an imagined future where the sway of the past wasn't so crushing, so absolute. I sat with the rest of my graduating class, some of whom had been with me the day of my injury six years before and had watched the ambulance approach the long weeds which had swallowed me up and the paramedics who had gone down into the ditch where I lay, broken and numb, staring up at the sky. That night we gathered in the middle of a football field, seated in folding chairs, listening to tepid bromides about the future, and our place in it, and what we should do and how we should live in order to shape that future. I wanted it to be over.

In the bleachers on both sides of the fields, family members fired cameras in the expanding darkness and hooted stupidly to fill up any pause or silence or moment in which we were not actively assured we would never be forgotten. That time held for us special affection and the sense that we'd never grow old, or at least no older than that night, or the bright morning after, or maybe the end of that Last Summer, When Real Life Begins.

From where I sat at the end of a row, tented in red regalia with a mortarboard clipped into my hair with barrettes, though I could feel it slipping back, I could see a young man in a wheelchair, older than me, seated by a fence. In his lap sat his girlfriend, and the whole ceremony they had kissed, their faces turned to give best access to their hunger.

Until my name was called and I had to roll over the uneven sod towards the twenty-foot-long ramp to the stage,

they held my interest, and then I forgot their queasy side-
show and went forward to receive my diploma. Bob Burnes
waited there with it, and when I reached the taped X on
the stage where we had been instructed to pause for a photograph I stopped, hearing applause stir in the crowd, but
thought of his promise and whether he'd mention it.

The photographer's cue and then his camera's starburst
froze us in tableau.

Bob Burnes said nothing but congratulations and my
name though beneath them both I sensed the pull of years
and a guilt that couldn't quite be assuaged.

chapter

ELEVEN

Early in my freshman year of college, I was mugged by a man who had followed me all morning long. Early to campus, I had time to waste, to blithely wander around in the autumn air, missing obvious clues he was tracking me, in and out of buildings, through parking lots and up ramps. He had even circled around me two times, passing by me on a sidewalk and then, later, waiting for me by a door, calling out to ask if I needed his help with it, even though I had been twenty feet from him and moving farther away each second. I thought nothing much of it, accustomed to the near-constant entreaties of strangers, though I should have known better.

■

We lived a few miles from a small state school; its presence forestalled any thoughts of leaving home for college, at least then, and the costs of living alone, paying out of pocket for health care attendants to bathe and dress me and at night return me to bed, were too great for the idea to take much root. Six years after breaking my neck, I was too accustomed to a compromised life, in which the usual choices were often out of reach, to feel any true regret. In truth, anyplace removed from the tedium of high school was an oasis.

I now had no one to write for me in the classes I took: Introduction to Music, Composition, and an algebra course so remedial I was unsure if I was attending by mistake. At first, this solitude felt strange, after six years of someone at my side. I fretted over notes: a *college* lecture was nothing like the rote recitations of high school, I was sure, and how could I retain it without notes? The thought of asking to borrow notes bothered me, as if it were borrowed money, a kind of debt I would be forced into. I waited, though, listening closely, reading carefully, and began to wonder if I had ever really required an assistant all those years. The freedom to be only myself, to engage with learning without any mediation, was a revelation. This place, and these pursuits, were my own, and would be in the future, I felt, and it was exhilarating.

But that morning, having arrived early, I went from the parking lot where my mother had dropped me off in our family's van, now equipped with a lift, to the campus student center. The cafeteria was empty and the frayed couches lining the hallways and lobby held nobody I knew. TVs mounted to the wall burbled faint streams of noise. I roamed the first floor, bored, hoping to see a classmate or even a professor.

There were two elevators in the building: one which rose to offices on the top floor, the other, located behind several heavy doors, which I had to push open with my wheelchair. The second elevator lowered into the building's basement. From the basement, untrafficked and dim except for a red emergency light, one could enter the campus game room where students played pool and Ping-Pong and fed quarters to a jukebox.

I knew a few students who would go down there, skipping classes, flirting with the girl behind the counter, who made change and rented the pool tables and hated her life, or her fate, whatever had landed her there, where it smelled like old cigarettes and burning tube socks. When I found no one I knew on the ground floor, I decided to take the elevator down to the game room. If nothing else, I could listen to the jukebox pouring out bad music or watch desultory bouts of Ping-Pong. Game, set, match.

The labyrinth of hallways leading to the elevator was empty but damp, like a sauna the world forgot. I pushed through the heavy doors and traveled down a long hallway, past steaming kitchens and carts burdened by pastries and boxed lunches and carafes of coffee and tea. I wanted more than anything to see someone who would in return be glad to see me.

At the elevator, I jabbed the down button with the mouth stick I always carried with me and waited for its doors to open. A tinny bell rang after a moment, and inside the rarely used car I went. The buttons were hard to reach, and I had to lean forward to reach them as the doors began to slide shut. But then the elevator car lurched, and the doors slid open again.

Someone else had entered. I pushed the down button again, after stretching out to reach it. The car began to descend after its doors sealed us in.

Over my right shoulder, behind me I could see a young man. When I recognized him, I froze. His hand was already deep inside my backpack, where the furious rustle of his hands was plain. I didn't want to antagonize him or escalate the situation. So far removed from the rest of the building, no one would hear if I called out for help and no one would come.

I pretended not to notice what was happening—I sat there as we descended, eyes pressed shut.

He found my wallet, a cheap green Mickey Mouse wallet given to me one Christmas by my twin brothers. In the elevator's brushed steel, through one half-opened eye, I could see his blurry hand hide my wallet in his jacket.

The doors opened and I backed my wheelchair out of the car, so scared I crashed against the side of it. I just wanted out.

He was holding the doors open for me.

"You OK, buddy?" he asked. "You sure you've got it?"

Scared, addled, surprised by his speaking, I had no idea what to say.

"No, no, I've got it," I said. "I'm OK."

chapter

TWELVE

His front teeth were missing, and livid, alluvial bruises spread down from his eyes, and he sat behind a table stacked with new copies of the undergraduate student literary journal. I assumed he had been beaten up, viciously battered to the point it hurt me to look at him, but I wanted to know his other secret: how I might be admitted into a poetry workshop, or help with production of the journal. I wanted to belong to a group I was still learning how to define. I wanted to know what that belonging meant. At the dim horizon of what seemed to me like my future, I could see what a writer's life was like, and more than anything that life was what I wanted.

Looking over the copies, covers in black and white, the lithe figure of a woman's back curving back into shadow, I tried to formulate something cogent. I waited around a long time while he sketched absently on notebook paper, less interested in art than in passing the time. Whorls of ink bloomed and divagated from margin to margin. Finally, I was ready to say something, all nerves and sweaty twitch.

"Are these free?" I asked, the best I could manage. He looked up at me, his face punched in, bloody.

"Yeah, take as many as you want," he mumbled.

I had expected to pay something for the copies, a few bucks at most, a dollar at least. Most of the poems inside had seemed fake, echoes of echoes, and hadn't interested me. But a few poems, weird and surreal, felt like they carried inside of them the spark of something true.

"Really?" I asked, taken aback. I wanted to befriend him, or at least introduce myself in some way. "I've wanted to get a copy since I saw the cover on a flyer."

He nodded, kind, but not especially interested.

"How do you get into the poetry workshop?" I blurted. "How do you do that? What do I need to do? Or who do I talk to to get permission?"

"Uh, you just sign up." He blinked. "Like any other class. When it's time to enroll. You sign up. That's all."

That it was no more complicated than that felt like a bit of a letdown. In my mind, I had been certain it would be difficult, a trial of signatures and permissions. Meetings in dank, book-strewn offices with professors who had no idea who I was and didn't care very much and chances to prove to them how much poetry meant to me and what I hoped to find within it, and, most importantly, within myself.

I had been writing poems in satisfying furies: the carriage of the typewriter I used for homework at home shuttled back and forth across the page with every line. Tactile, immediate, typing introduced me to the pleasure of creating, of making. I had no idea what a poet might be, or do, but I knew I wanted to be one, and would do whatever it took.

That first workshop was filled with recognizable types: the gothic, draped in black; the ingénue; and the affably oafish fraternity brother, looking for an easy A, at least at first, until stirred by something unexpected (in this case, he would disappear just before semester's end, only to reappear in the police blotter, accused of rape); others who dabbled, who wrote in journals, who had been encouraged by family members to follow their smatter of talent; and me, the true believer, the one mad for it all, borrowing Whitman and Ginsberg and Denis Johnson like I had been starved, the one who shadowed professors with new poems and the crazy belief that it all mattered, that it was important, that it was transformative, that this was romantic and true. I couldn't escape the notion that I was alone, in a broken body, stuck in the places between that body and everyone else, and that maybe each word and every line and all the poems I wrote were a tether, a rope by which I could hang on to the world, and not be left behind entirely, which I feared more than anything.

In a Viking history class I met a girl named Mona, her voice the twirl and lilt of some rural, unknown place. She was short and dark-haired and solicitous in a kind way; she was always early to class, the first to arrive, sitting in a desk beside the door. Every day when I entered class she spoke, bright eyes and syrupy twang. It was no time before a crush on her had gripped me, though I said nothing of it when we began to chat before class. Music, movies, the Vinland Sagas we were parsing our way through—whatever I could think of to continue the tenuous strand of conversation between strangers. I would arrive at class as early as I could, even as I derided myself for being so obvious, so pathetic. Still, two days a week I hurried through crowds of students, who barely could be bothered to part, to one side or the other. Once, racing through rain, I slid from the sidewalk, into mud, and my tires shed red clay all that miserable day.

The professor was balding, snaggletoothed, sublimely acerbic. His hands gripped befouled coffee mugs like claws. He barked and guffawed and had no illusions that I was somehow delicate, grunting my last name.

Mona sat two rows over from me in the narrow class-room, one seat back. Always a flutter in my peripheral vision, she took notes that seemed to capture every syllable in wiry loops of ink. If I didn't stare straight ahead, she'd be there, a feathered blur at the edge of my sight. I tried to bore my eyes into the wall, the tattered map of America's topography unspooled beside the murky chalkboard.

Still, there were days when I had no interest in the knobby spine of the Appalachian mountains and let myself watch her. Her studiousness, which seemed to seep the air from my lungs. There was a day I learned nothing when she applied lotion to her darkened legs, oblivious, intent. Another day when, passing through a parking lot, I stumbled on her in her car, furtively changing out of her workout clothes. For a moment all I could see was hurried, undifferentiated skin, a blur which took my breath.

Over time we became friends. Nothing more would come of it. Entering class one day, I spoke to Mona, as always, but noticed a young girl, six or seven, in a desk beside her, coloring spare paper with outsized boredom. Mona introduced me to her daughter, who didn't look up from her crayons until scolded. I said hello but my eyes had gone instead to Mona's left hand, where there was now a simple wedding band. And always had been. In my naiveté, I'd never considered that she might be married. That surprise must have been evident.

"I bet you didn't know I had a little girl," she said, her face amused.

"I didn't even know you were married."

Mona paused a moment, tapping her pen. Her daughter had returned to coloring.

"Oh, yes," she replied, not sad, not wistful, not any single emotion, looking out a window, but not really. "Since I was fifteen."

The story was too familiar, too obvious, to be further surprised: older boyfriend, pregnancy, small-town scandal, forced wedding. Alongside that narrative, my own foolishness played out, weeks of mooning for what I could not have.

In some ways, we grew closer, as if this last bit of elided biography had prevented any friendship beyond that of the casual acquaintance. As if she'd brought her daughter along rather than speak of her existence.

And, yet, in that closeness, in which we continued to talk, had lunch, occasionally studied, I withdrew, willing to be a friend, to listen, to be an ear receptive to her long unhappiness. I was kind and patient and, above all, present. She could open her heart to me because I was safe, incapable of acting.

I nursed a kind of bitterness and was ashamed. I listened and spoke and tried to craft consolation from whatever I could, whatever I had, which didn't feel like much.

Mona knew where I lived with my family and sometimes would call if nearby to see if she could drop in. She would bring lunch from a fried fish house nearby, which had a bus-sized catfish in its front lawn. Battered cod or shrimp, hush puppies that sweated grease into their cardboard containers. Taught to be polite, I always ate the food, which was either awful or sublime or both all at once, depending on how little you cared for the integrity of your heart.

The following summer, after Viking history, Mona appeared once more at our home. Outside, everything broiled beneath a pane of faded-out sky. She asked if she could take a swim in our pool, out behind our house. The moment felt wrong or warped but I said why not, that she could change in the bathroom.

She wanted to talk, even through the door, which left me beside it to listen and respond. A minute or two passed. She announced she was coming out.

Mona stepped out in a two-piece swimsuit the color of foamed milk. The curls of her hair were tied up in a chestnut haze. Her top covered her breasts entirely, or would have, if not for the mesh pane between them, and the freckled skin it exposed.

Mona walked down the hallway into the living room, where the door to the back porch and steps down to the pool were located. She hadn't said a word. My mother was watching television in the living room while knitting.

Mona waved to my mother before opening the door, before speaking to me.

"Do you like my swimsuit, Paul?"

I nodded dumbly and followed her out to the heat and the water and the stage of her loneliness. I watched her laze through the water, dipping under its lacquered surface, laughing like a child. In that heat, I couldn't follow any conversation. Due to my quadriplegia, I was susceptible to sunstroke. Too long in that light would leave me weak, the sound of my blood in my ears, spots of light flecking my sight. As she swam, I tried not to reach that point.

When I had retreated to shadow thrown from the roof's eave, Mona lifted herself from the pool and covered herself with a beach towel. It was time, she said, that she go. She would be late to pick up her daughter. In her clothes again, by my bedroom door, Mona seemed sad. My body couldn't cool. That was all that I cared—that was all that I wanted. And for her to go. To take nothing more.

chapter

THIRTEEN

"I don't know if I can leave you," my mother half sobbed the night before she drove home from Carbondale, Illinois, where I was about to begin graduate school, living on my own for the first time in my life. Her voice had flattened into anguish, a simple, sad O. Quickly, as quickly as it had erupted, she pushed the fear back, palming away the tears which ran in hot strands down her face. I was in bed already, the same hospital-style bed I had slept in for ten years, in a small apartment across the street from a law school and beside a lake which was already filling with leaves as fall came on.

Ten years had taught me no better how to be cried over.

Which was a form of mourning, long distended. I thought of my father, in the days following my surgery, when I'd felt like something emptied and then filled again with pain, and how he had sobbed beneath the weight of love and its unbreakable responsibility. Then, I'd been a child, saved from pain for that moment by his. Whatever fear I felt now, in Illinois, on the eve of my independent life, became concern for her, though that hardly gave me the right words to speak.

"I'm going to be all right," I said. "I will."

I looked away. Though I believed what I said, I had no way of guaranteeing it. No way of seeing into the uncertain three years while I completed a master's in fine arts. All I could say had been said. It was late now and we were tired, ready for sleep, even though we'd say good-bye in the morning. I shut my eyes.

She had been in Illinois with me for two weeks while we looked for someone to assist me every day, and after a long run of candidates who had never worked in health care before, were not even sure of the work I wanted them to do, or those who had, who wanted jobs which would pay them to look after me the entire day and through the night, as if I had dementia, and swore to my mother I wouldn't escape their all-seeing eyes. No one, no one, seemed right, and privately I think we worried no one would suit my needs. Then, after another day of calling strangers, numbers and names given to us by motley sources, a man answered brusquely, in a hurry, just at the edge of impatience. He spoke with what I guessed was an Eastern European accent.

"Yes, yes, what is it?" he said loudly. A woman yelled in the background and I was silent while he yelled back. "What do you want? Who is calling me today?"

He spoke quickly, almost too quickly to follow, his words smashing up against one another, but in an oddly formal way, with surplus verbiage scattered throughout. Every sentence rose to a little giggle, as if its true meaning were a secret amusement.

I explained to him what I needed and what I didn't need. He interrupted me.

"I did this," he barked. "Do not fear: I am your man!"

I paused a second, closing my eyes. He would be the one. I was certain, rueful, intrigued. "You've worked with quadriplegics before?"

"Many!" he shouted, excited. "Yes. I know how to remove your urine and your poop and none of this bothers me."

The way he said *poop* was either charming or insane: delicate, yet high-speed, not quite aware of how truly strange he sounded. How plosive and boyish.

I looked over to my mother, who read on the couch. She listened to us on the speakerphone, smiling but determinedly looking down at the page lest she break into her own fit of giggling. She waved her hand at me, wanting no part. I asked him to come over that evening.

His knock pounded into the metal door like machine gun fire. *Blamblamblam.* He was nearly through the door before it had opened, his head swiveling around, his arm clapping me on the back, smacking hard. My skin stung for minutes. He was short, but thick with bands of muscle. His hair bristled, dark black and full of gray, as was the mustache which rested on his lip like an enormous caterpillar. He wore zebra-print jogging pants, a fanny pack around his waist, and an aqua muscle shirt from which a thatch of robust chest hair sprang.

"Hello, hello, hello," he half-shouted, taking my mother's hand in his own before kissing it lightly, bowing comically, his arm extended behind him in grand flourish.

He introduced himself as Lazar Tonu, said I should call him Tony, from Romania, most recently employed on the riverboats in Metropolis, where gambling was legal, as a janitor. His wife, whom he met in a karate class, was Japanese. He went on.

"Are you curious how I speak so well your language?" he asked. "I can assure you we were never taught it in school."

His eyes bounced back and forth between us, measuring our interest, clearly excited to have an audience for his tale.

"Oh, of course," I said, trying not to look at my mother.

"I tell you," he said, leaning closer, inviting us into something secret. "At night, I would enter a library through a window in the roof that was broken. No one knew that it was as good as a door if you climbed to the top. No one knew. But I knew."

This was important to him. His index finger shot up and he pointed to his chest.

"That's something else," my mother said. I glared at her.

"I knew," he continued. "At night I crept in through this window and I hid with books I could not read and books that I could read and all night long I remained this way. Night after night. Risking discovery. Until I had taught myself English."

He paused to let it sink in for us before going on. We were quiet.

"And when I could read, I made my plans," he whispered, an air of the conspirator about him. My mother had begun to be drawn in, I could see, and so had I. Despite his cartoon absurdity, his Wile E. Coyote machinations, he possessed an inexplicable hint of gravitas and couldn't be entirely dismissed. He leaned even farther out from his chair, adjusting his fanny pack, eyeing us.

"I watched and waited," he confided. "For many months, I watched and waited, biding my time."

I began to worry about what he had waited for.

"And then when the signs were good and no moon was in the sky . . ." He paused, relishing the moment. "In the darkness I swam the river Danube and escaped my country Romania."

He sat back in his chair, smoothing his zebra-print

sweatpants with his palms, and waited for me to hire him, who had also lived through much.

Later that night Tony announced himself with his signature attack on my door. I let him in, smiling to see the same zebra stripes, the same fanny pack ringing his hips. He seemed to be all energy, all enthusiasm.

"Are you ready to fly?" he asked, switching from foot to foot, like a sprinter preparing for a race. I had no clue what he was talking about.

"I usually transfer from my chair to my bed by standing," I said. "With your help. With your arms under mine like you were giving me a hug. You know what I mean, right?"

I asked this hopefully. He scrutinized me, jittery.

"I like to do this in another way," he replied. "Will you let me try? I am strong. Do not worry."

He twisted his fanny pack around to his back, widened the stance of his legs, then clapped his hands loudly. I winced.

"Are you ready to fly?" he asked, looking me in the eyes. He waited for me to say something, I realized. "You must say it. Say that you are ready."

I just stared at him, then relented. "Yes," I said. "Yes, I'm ready to fly."

"Come to mama!"

He scooped me up in his arms like a small child, holding me to his chest, and ran from my wheelchair in the middle of the room to my bed, where he dropped me on to the mattress like a professional wrestler. He giggled, pleased with himself.

"I didn't expect you to do that, Tony," I said, a little stunned, bemused by this odd man. It was important to him that I be impressed by his strength and, in truth, I was, having been lifted up and sprinted to bed like a participant in an Olympic event that never made the cut. His eyes, small and bright, flickered with obvious delight. He rubbed his hands together, ready to prove himself in some other way.

"You see," he said, as if inviting me into knowledge that very few might ever possess, "there is no weight so great that I cannot lift it."

I smiled, or tried to. I depended on him now. I needed him. I was his weight, his proof of strength and mastery.

After months Tony had not changed: everything he said bore the weight of revelation and still he insisted on scooping me up in his arms every night like a frenzied parent running from a burning home. He always wore the same clothes, the same fanny pack, and would call his wife from my phone, engaging in long, twisting disagreements that seemed to resolve nothing. When he hung up, he would stand for a little while at my windows, absently pushing his hands through his coarse hair, and when he turned back to me, its disarray was sad.

"My wife forbids me to drink soda," he would say at night. "Might I have one?"

His eyes, always a little wild, took on a burdened aspect. He would sit in front of me while he pensively sipped Pepsi. Soon, he began bringing his own stashes of forbidden items: soda, chocolate, potato chips. He hid them in my closet, retrieving something every night with boyish glee.

When he learned that I wrote poetry, he would expound at length on the poverty of modern art, and poetry in particular, that it had abandoned rhyme and meter and all the other pleasures that were characteristic of truly great poetry.

"Why can poetry no longer rhyme," he asked intently, "and what good is all its darkness? Morbid, morose—no good! I tell you, the greatest poet of Romania only writes of graveyards and children who have died too soon! Who says that he is great? I do not!"

By then, I had learned how to exist inside one of his conversations, which was to agree or disagree as deftly as possible, saying little, listening more than anything.

That winter I tore a tendon in my right ankle, falling out of my wheelchair in the parking lot outside my apartment. I lay there, the night sky whirling above me, until two male students found me and lifted me back into my chair. My ankle throbbed.

Inside, I called Tony. He arrived quickly, bounding into my apartment, but his face was framed by concern. He looked me over.

"You have been drinking, have you?" he asked darkly.

"I don't drink, Tony," I replied. "You know that. Get this shoe off me?"

My right foot was swelling already. I groaned.

Tony looked at me, thinking hard, running his hand through his hair. He went to my refrigerator for ice, filling a plastic bag. He helped me into bed, elevating my foot, applying ice.

Tony, preoccupied, muttered to himself. At last, he looked to me.

"May I use your phone?"

"Well, yeah, sure, be my guest," I said. I was irritated that he wanted to call someone.

He dialed, waited, his face tense. He placed his hand over the receiver.

"I pray that we do not wake my wife," he said, winking. "Hello? Hello. Yes. Were you sleeping?"

His face darkened. He turned away, as though I would be shielded from the heated words with his back to me. He reached back, giving me a thumbs-up. He waited for a few moments, humming to himself. Minutes passed. Finally he began to speak.

"Hello? Hello?"

Another moment passed. He began to speak once more, not in English and not in Japanese. I guessed it might be Romanian.

When Tony left, he would only say that he would return very quickly, that I should not be concerned. Before I could question him, he had gone, his manic urgency multiplied by an unknown factor. The ice bag fell from my ankle. I wished he had turned off the light so I could try to rest. I wondered how long it would be before he returned, if he would return at all. My leg began to spasm sharply.

Before long there was a light knock at my door. Tony unlocked the door with his key, stepping inside. He spoke to someone outside then waved him in.

A tiny man, shorter than Tony, ancient-looking, slowly walked in. He wore a drab winter coat and a hat with fur-ringed flaps over the ears. He carried a weathered leather satchel.

That's his father, I thought.

"He does not speak English," Tony said.

"And you brought him here— Why is he here?"

"My father, he is an old man," Tony said, "and he knows the old ways still. He has a gift."

"A gift for what?"

"For *healing*," he said quietly, almost whispering. "It is of the Lord."

"Yeah," I said, wishing I could vanish.

"It involves fire," he said, gravely serious.

A weird fascination was beginning to take hold. When Tony had said *fire*, his father nodded vigorously, making a gesture like a flame leaping up from his palm.

"Fire," I repeated. Father and son nodded in unison.

"It is an old way of healing," he said. "My father will take a special oil and place it on your skin. Where you have injured your ankle."

"Uh-huh."

"He will ignite that oil." Tony grinned. "Then he will extinguish it with a glass cup. This will draw the pain from you."

"By setting me on fire."

His father made the vaguely explosive fire gesture again. He opened the satchel he was carrying, retrieving a small cup, not much larger than a shot glass, and began to speak to me in Romanian. Tony translated.

"My father says you will be very safe."

His father continued to speak.

"My father says there is very little pain. He says that it will leave red marks. But they will go away."

"Good to know."

There was a part of me, the boy still in me, who loved

fire and the fireworks my grandfather kept, that was curious to see this shrunken old man practice his gift on me. But even that curiosity could not change the reality of the moment: that two Romanian men, a father and son, stood beside my bed well after midnight calmly discussing how best to safely set fire to my skin.

"Actually, Tony," I interjected. "I don't think I'm up for anything involving self-immolation—"

"Self-what?" Tony asked, puzzled.

"Immolation. It's—it's like ritualistically setting yourself on fire."

"Who would do such a thing?"

"That's my whole point."

I could tell that refusing him might be an insult. I tried to think of some way to politely refuse. They waited for me to say more.

"My injury," I said earnestly. "My body is different."

"Your quadriplegia."

"Right."

"I had not considered this," Tony said, looking abashed.

I saw that I had reached him. They whispered to each other.

"Forgive me, but my father has requested something."

"Yes?"

"He has asked if he may pray for you."

The wizened old man, his fur-lined hat still on his head, knelt painfully. He brought his gnarled hands together.

■

To depend on someone else for everything you cannot do for yourself, no matter how private, is to cultivate a forced intimacy. To engage in this with Tony, who carried me in his arms like a child, who announced himself as *mama* when he did, was to invite indignity after indignity. It was a compact struck with myself, with the fact of my injury, made to enlarge my life. Even so, there were moments when the cost of that new independence was almost too much to bear. One night, when I was about to bathe, seated in a shower chair which rolled on small caster wheels, I was wearing only a white T-shirt and one sock. Tony stood beside me, folding the day's clothes while the cascade of shower water warmed.

Before I realized what was happening, he had dropped my clothes on the floor, and was pushing past me in the cramped bathroom, rushing to the toilet. Before sitting down, his face twisted in pain, he paused for a moment, as if he realized that I was still there, half naked in a chair my arms couldn't push from the bathroom, as if he were searching for an adequate apology. There wasn't one. He dropped his zebra-striped sweatpants and sat down, eyes on me.

His bowels emptied into my toilet, less than three feet from me, liquid, explosive, unending. Facing him, I couldn't look away.

When Tony was finished, he flushed and leaped up,

clapping me hard on my shoulder, a wild grin on his face.

"I guess," he laughed, "that the honeymoon is over!"

When my mother left Illinois, when she left me to begin an independent life, she drove for six hours, past rivers and rolling sheets of bluegrass and mountains dissolving into hills, back to Georgia, where she had always lived. How hard that was I'm left to imagine, and in this, despite every poem I have written and every book I have published, I fail. From the sidewalk, I watched her go, gripped by the sadness of good-bye but exhilarated by everything before me, all of it unknown.

Inside, as a motorized door opener drew my door silently shut, I looked about my little apartment. The blue couch beside the door and the long L-shaped desk beside it, on which my computer slept. Two walls with high windows looking out on to a lawn where ROTC students would later march, calling cadence in the snow. My bed, an electric hospital bed like the one I had slept in for ten years, with a switch on a flexible armature that controlled the lights, the door, and a radio on the windowsill for times when pain would wake me and hold me back from the brink of sleep. A small bathroom but one I could enter in my wheelchair.

It was mine, at least for a time, and thinking this, as alone as I was, I smiled.

chapter

FOURTEEN

I did not like her. Not when we first met, in class, and
she talked nervously, blurting jagged bolts of talk, laughing loudly, pulling everyone's attention to her, even as she
seemed not to want it. To prefer quietly attending the tides
of discussion, without being dragged into them. I knew how
that felt, could be empathetic, but here she was, unable
to stop laughing at wan jokes, smacking her hands on the
table so that papers and books rattled with every percus-
sive snort, and, when discussing someone's work, exclaim-
ing her own worries. Tall, with hair pragmatically cut, well
dressed but unfussy, Lydia left quickly after our first poetry
workshop, disappearing, as if she might not return.

■

During the day, if I was with no one I knew, I ate by myself, ordering a sandwich from one of the fast-food places in the student center. After asking an employee to carry it for me to a table, preferably one far from others because I hated the sensation of strange watchfulness that would fall on me as I ate, I leaned over to the plate, taking a bite. I could see that some thought it sad, pitied me, but it was enlightening to exist this way, learning how I could be capable on my own, learning how best to function in solitude.

Lydia was eating an open-faced ham sandwich when I saw her again and she waved me over to where she sat against a wall. For a moment I hesitated, reluctant to go over, to talk to someone who had so frankly annoyed me on that first night of class. But I went, knowing I needed friends and wanted them, and though there was an unexpected ex- hilaration that came over me every night when Tony would leave, turning off all the lights, I knew that it could only last so long, that feeling, and beyond it would be astringent loneliness, which slowly reached your core, your heart, and would not go, static as stone and as heavy. To be paralyzed was to first be estranged from your own body, a loneliness which would always be with you. To be estranged from the bodies of others was the next and greater danger.

"Would you like to share this?" she asked, her mouth chewing. "There's plenty. There's too much. I can't eat it all."

I considered. There is an awkwardness involved when I eat with someone for the first time, depending on them to feed me each bite. Parallel to that runs an inescapable intimacy. I have to judge the person and the situation; I never want to make another person feel uncomfortable. Many times I've claimed I wasn't hungry if I felt like the person had not thought about what I would need. Lydia smiled sweetly.

"How can I turn down a— What exactly is that?"

"It's an open-faced ham sandwich," she said, her voice still thick with sandwich. "I love them. Call me crazy, but I do."

"Well, sign me up."

We ate and talked and soon were laughing. We gossiped about our classmates, the beanpole classic rock maestro and the soft-spoken philosophy major who carried fragrant tobacco with him for his pipe. We complained about the ones who said nothing and the ones we wished would say nothing. Soon the lunch we'd shared was gone and with it the time. We decided to meet again the following week.

A few charged weeks passed this way: lunch, e-mail, the phone. I felt heavy with longing, as though the air were lead. I had no idea what to do. The phone rang one night in November while I worked on a poem at my desk. I answered.

"Can I come by?" Lydia asked. "I'm at the library making copies."

When she arrived, she came with bags, books, food. We ate, listening to music. Lydia lay on the floor, on her back, beside my old stereo.

I turned to where she was, now sitting up, her back against my couch. She began to play with the leather laces of my shoes, too long, forever untied. She tugged at one of them, drawing it out. It reached to her waist where she tied it loosely through a belt loop. She untied the lace and slipped my shoes off before returning to the floor, stretched out.

I turned to her, leaning over, looking down. Her eyes were closed. I didn't know what to do. With as much dexterity as I could manage, I extended my leg, running my foot over hers. Her eyes remained closed when I reached her waist, her stomach, massaging her. She was quiet and still. I was unsure of what was transpiring, if I was even ready.

She had on a gauzy white button-down shirt. I traced its meridian of buttons upward. No longer so nervous, I touched her right breast, tentatively, waiting to see that she did not resist.

"Come here," I whispered. She opened her eyes. Getting up, she looked to my door, leaning back against it, her hand on the knob. She was thinking of leaving.

She said something soundless, just breath. I leaned slightly into her, kissing the arm closest to me. But she leaned into me. We kissed, there against the door, for the first time. I forgot my fears. There was only her.

When that kiss had ended, long and sweet, when we pulled slightly apart from one another, when I looked up into her face and the hair that had fallen across her face, all my words were of no use. An ease had fallen over us, an acceptance. Neither of us shook. We were not scared. She smiled sweetly and I knew that I loved her. I kissed her hand.

She led me to the couch where she sat, staring off, working through something unspoken. I let her think, saying nothing. She reached for the lamp beside the couch, dimming it. The room fell into a burnished dimness. She looked at me.

"Can I ask you something?" she said.

"Of course."

"Would you mind . . ." She paused. "Would you like to lie down with me? Can I take off your pants?"

A shyness had returned to her. It melted me. I kissed her once more. She helped me to stand from my chair. For the first time, we were eye to eye. Lydia helped me to sit, then to lie back on the couch, just wide enough for both of us. It would become the place where we would always go, my bed too narrow, uncomfortable, not right.

Her hands unfastened the button of my jeans, slipping them down my legs and off me. She laid them neatly across the back of my chair. Next was my shirt, tossed to the side.

Her clothes fell away from her in a clump. I watched her watch me.

We nearly fell when she came to me, when we began. Our bodies slid from the low couch halfway onto the floor. We laughed, kissing, moving back, slow, her body atop mine, covering me like a blanket. Her hair fell around my face. She wore a perfume I didn't know.

I loved her as best as I was able, given the paucity of my experience, a form of immaturity which led me into mistakes and misunderstandings and misreadings: confusions which, in the course of our time together, broke us apart. When we argued, I felt like I was sprinting through hip-high water, impossibly slowed, saying the wrong things, again and again and again. All my life had been spent reading books and writing poems and these were not the same as reading a person's concerns, fears, insecurities. For three years, the length of my studies in graduate school, we flailed, trying, failing, apart as much as we were together.

We said good-bye beneath trees beside the lake. Dogwood petals fluttered in the air. The next day I left Illinois and I felt smaller and sadder than I ever had.

chapter

FIFTEEN

When I came to Tuscaloosa, to the University of Alabama, with three years of poems, the chill of Midwestern winter, and the sting of loss still fresh, I had no idea what I would do except teach and, once more, try to create a home for myself where none was. I knew no one, no one but a professor named Dana Ream who had invited me to teach there, when we met following a reading I'd given in Chattanooga, where I lived with my parents following graduate school. In the weeks before I moved, I would dream of parachuting into darkness, noise of a silken rip all around me. Whatever waited below, unseen and unknown, I fell toward it, unerring, a stone.

∎

My parents, the twins, and I left home early on the fifteenth of August with a U-Haul truck packed with my possessions. When we arrived in Tuscaloosa, it would be the nineteenth day in a row with temperatures above one hundred degrees. The air was hard to breathe, leaden with humidity. Nothing moved, or if it did, it moved like regret. The asphalt parking lots glittered, molten, tacky. I began to wonder if, maybe, this was a mistake.

In some ways I was right.

Down the sidewalk a man in an elephant costume dragged a rubber chicken behind him, its floppy, broken neck in a heavy rope noose. No one in the crowd seemed to think him strange: they hooted their approval, high-fived his other hand or hoof or whatever it was waving cheerfully. I followed him. It was the first home game of the football season. Expectation swept like a plague over everything and everyone. I had never been around anything like it. Winnebagos had begun cruising into town two days previous, on Thursday night, filling up parking lots normally ceded to students—who had to vacate or be towed. From my apartment I could see season ticket holders fire up countless gas-powered generators. The polyphonic buzz sounded like giant, burping armies of locusts. Wide-screen television sets and satellite dishes were erected in the lots, and full kitchens arrayed under the broad shade of magnolias.

I walked back to my cramped apartment with its weirdly stained carpet: dark splashes ringed the floor. I'd soon learn the previous tenant was a drunken, combative quadriplegic given to changing his colostomy bag anywhere he felt like it. He would dump his waste into a bucket in the hallway outside his door, beneath a hand-drawn biohazard symbol.

I only hoped my neighbors bothered to tell us apart.

My apartment building was ancient, heated and cooled by an arcane complex of vents which dumped so much moisture into the air that my bedsheets always felt damp and towels never fully dried. Drafts of poems on my desk would curl up and books would swell and bow, deformed by the air. I lived at the end of a long hall where once I awoke to the blurry murmurs of sex against my door: *You promised, you promised.*

On my first day of classes I set out early to find my way through the campus, jewel green, even in a drought, sprinklers kicking beads of water in long arcs through the air. The day was still cool and quiet. I felt good, absorbed with humming.

But a sidewalk ahead was busted up, blocking me from going further. In the near distance, the English department building glowed and faded as clouds passed above in the pewter sky. I turned around to enter the student center, to take its elevator to a level above the construction.

The electric door opener at the entrance had not been switched on so early in the day. I had to wait, either for staff inside the student center or for someone to happen along. I stared through my reflection in the wide glass doors, looking for a custodian, for security, gradually falling into a daydream.

Then there was a meaty arm draping my shoulder and a woman's rouge-splotchy face uncomfortably close to mine.

"Do you need help, young man?" she trilled, hugging me tight.

"I'm, uh, I'm waiting for someone to open that door," I said, flummoxed by this woman, heavy and pale, and too close.

"I'd be glad to help you with that. Would it bother you if I prayed for you? Do you believe in a risen savior?"

She positively radiated Jesus. I knew her type well. They flitted about in public like epileptic wrens, darting and swerving and praying like Pharisees.

"Sure," I said, hoping that was the path of least resistance, the quickest escape.

"Lord, he is determined. We see in him the same determination with which you created the sun and stars and the earth and moon. Bless him, Lord. Bless him."

I winced, wanting away.

"Can I tell you something?" she asked, her face floating in like a cheap planet.

"OK."

"You're beautiful!"

Her lips mashed to my cheek, hot and smeary. In my head, I began a startled, anxious prayer of my own. I said nothing.

"Open that door," she said, nodding to her right. I turned my head.

Her son, I guessed, slablike and impassive, tall and seemingly narcoleptic, swayed from one foot to the other. She whistled, shrill and high, into my ear and at him. He sprang towards the door and I went after him, fleeing.

Receding into the distance, she sang out, "Maybe I'll see you around sometime!"

I only accelerated, faster and farther from her and her blessing.

Nothing felt quite right in Tuscaloosa, even in the early days: the buses had no lifts, leaving me stranded on the island of the campus and its surroundings. I roamed, trying to acquaint myself, finding shuttered businesses and men on corners with evangelical broadsides. Once, a young man, barely twenty, swallowed up by his suit, sweating in the heat, offered me one, crumpled in his hand like an old dollar bill. I looked at him, at his hand.

"What's it about?" I asked, though I knew the number

by heart. His entire body paused—for an instant, it ceased to move. The question confounded him.

"It's—" he stammered, stunned to have been acknowledged. "It's about, you know, um, it's about Satan."

"No, thanks," I said, going on my way, before he could recover himself, before he could hurry after me, his pamphlets forgotten, asking if he could pray for me, right there on the sidewalk, in the shadow of a liquor store.

The poem that became the first poem in my first book began as an error.

I had misread an entry in an immense dictionary that the English department kept in its narrow mailroom. I could only wedge myself in far enough to page through the yellowed book. A kind of thrill took me one day, scanning down a random page, when I read that melancholia, in Middle English, meant *black hole*. The sense of that etymology, its essential rightness, sparked all through my brain. This was a poem, I thought. And it was, but not the one unfolding in my imagination like a sheet of hammered silver, bright and friable.

I looked at the entry a second time. I'd misread *hole*—the real meaning was *bile*. Black bile. At first, all I could think of were dark bodily secrets, the gall bladder impacted with strange, salty stones. An acid stream in the mouth.

My disappointment faded as that error in reading took

on its own loveliness, its own allusive possibilities. This is the poem, I thought. Lines were already lying down in rows in my mind. I could see them, almost.

I hurried out of the office and out of the building. I feared I'd lose the poem if I couldn't type it out, that I'd never find it again. Failed poems came to mind, ones I had thought about in the middle of the night, unable to sleep, and with no ability to reach for a notebook and pen or a laptop glowing warmly. As much as was possible I rushed home, trying to hold it all in, past friends and past buildings I saw every day and past trees I often stopped beneath for a little while when it was too hot to walk anywhere.

The automatic entrance to my building worked only half the time, often leaving me stuck outside, waiting for someone to exit, to hold the door. With the poem still uncoiling, I prayed the door would open for me. It did. Inside, at my computer, I began to type what I already had written, nine or ten lines, and after I had, the rest was easy.

The poem, titled "Melancholia," seemed to me to be all blue, pewter specked with cloud white. Flash Gordon rocketed about, and Petrarch was name-checked, and behind it all thrummed a new sort of love, a new competence, a deeper engagement with the world and my own feelings. This was different, better, truer than all the poems I'd written before. Looking at the screen, rereading the lines, I felt changed.

New as well was teaching. Throughout graduate school,

I'd avoided the pressed labor of the teaching assistantship, awarded a fellowship which gave me all the time I could have wanted but none of the experience. I was nervous going into my first class, which met in an all-glass room beside a bathroom. Toilets flushed and flushed, sounding like arrhythmic surf. Battered metal blinds half-hid the constant procession but the seepage of cell phone talk was without end.

My students came from places like Montgomery and Mobile and Birmingham and Opelika and Sylacauga. They seemed to have little sense of the history which had broiled around them for decades. When I announced one morning that the Alabama State Legislature had voted to repeal laws barring miscegenation, older than any of them and older than me, it was hard not to see them for the children they still were. Bright but still unformed. One boy, bluff and soft everywhere, little eyes swallowed up by his face, confided in me his difficulties: he'd had to learn how to operate an alarm clock, wake himself up every morning, that his mama had always done this.

Small, quiet, draped in the echoes of bad history, Tuscaloosa never felt like it could be a home for me. I would travel in my chair from the campus into town, which looked deserted at night, newly abandoned, the staging ground of the Rapture, when Jesus is said to return, lifting believers up into the air. More than one car in Tuscaloosa bore bumper stickers about the Rapture, and in the heavy, humid nights, while I searched side streets limned by massive magnolias, I thought about the Rapture. About being called up into the air, in an instant, all the cars assured me. About the new body that was promised to believers, as soon as check-in in Heaven began. Whenever that was. I thought of my own body.

I think I was never so alone as those nights in Tuscaloosa, where I tried to find my way. From campus to a grocery store. To anywhere. The dark would unfurl and choirs of cicadas would begin to sing out. Their noise was like a second night.

The first time I heard Eliot Khalil Wilson read, I loved him, I felt I'd found an older brother, with hair that refused a comb, glasses that thickened each year. His wardrobe wasn't so much vintage as it was reclaimed from Goodwill. He was tall, and a near-constant profusion of sweat beaded his forehead.

The English department held readings in a natural science museum auditorium down the street. Its elevator was walled off behind glass, sequestered, and no one could use it without the proper codes. The night Eliot read, no one who knew those codes was around. I waited in the marble lobby, exasperated. I thought about going home. Upstairs, I heard the readers begin. I wanted to leave then, in limp protest, but outside, rain whipped the sidewalks and tore limbs from the trees. At last, the bearer of codes arrived, soaked and foul-tempered, stabbing at the keys with her damp finger.

I tried to sneak into the auditorium. The audience, with its hive mind, turned toward me. I smiled, nodded, willed invisibility.

At the podium, Eliot and a woman stood, alternately reading passages from an essay about food. He spoke of his diabetes, the dangers to his health, and of what he often dreamed at night: an undulant river of chocolate, his body falling from a great height into it, sinking into sugared coma like a millstone.

It was deadpan virtuosity, and little of the crowd seemed to get it. The effect was baroque and madcap and bracing, all at once. I thought of syringes and blood and an ever-deepening blindness. And I laughed.

Walking home after the reading, when the rain had passed on, toward Birmingham and then Atlanta, I thought, *I will be crushed if we aren't friends.*

I clung to that hope, that wish for friendship, connection, anything.

The humid weather of my apartment drove me from it. I would see any movie, no matter how bad, at a nearby theater. I needed out, away.

Late autumn in Tuscaloosa was still warm, with a giant slab sky overhead and stars that seemed to run like butter in a pan. One night, I went my slow way down the sidewalks and past the parking lots and up a long ramp into the theater.

Slumped down beside me, a green jacket pulled tightly around her, was a girl I'd seen in the company of English graduate students. Her name was Ivy. She taught in the biology department, working on a Ph.D. in genetics. I said hello. We chatted until the lights went down. Before long, the film caught in the projector's gate, melting. Slowly, everyone filed out but us.

We stayed a long while, talking about mutual friends, campus politics, movies, or books we'd recently read. When it was late and the building closed, I went with her to her car. She paused.

"Let me give you a hug," she said, sweetly.

That night at home, I was uncertain of how I felt. Nothing about the encounter was galvanic, charged. I wondered if I should contact her again. After a few days had passed, I searched out her e-mail address and suggested we get together again. She agreed, answering from the lab she rarely left.

Ivy was shy and often intractable, sensitive and sullen, working fifteen-hour days culturing unicellular organisms, swabbing petri dishes, ruining her green eyes. I delivered lunch to her, salads, sandwiches, then returned to my classes.

More dates followed. Rented movies, ordered pizza. I tried to nurse her exhaustion. I wrote my poems.

After several weeks, we had only kissed—she was Catholic, devout, a virgin, and our relationship never grew urgent with the imperative of sex. I told myself I was respecting her beliefs, and this was true, but the truth I couldn't face was my own disengagement, the last, lingering effects of heartbreak, carried there from Illinois.

At night, while my attendant helped me to bathe, undress, lie down in the bed I carried from state to state, she would wait in her car in the parking lot of the football stadium. When my attendant left, I'd call her cell phone and then she'd drive to my apartment, letting herself in with a spare key.

She never turned on a light. She would slip from her clothes, and crawl into the narrow twin bed, where we'd lie, naked until the morning.

Once, on a freezing night, when she wore to bed an old T-shirt, I kissed her breasts through the worn fabric.

"I don't see why you do that," she said quietly. "It doesn't feel like anything."

And so I turned away, pressing against the bed's metal rail.

■

One night, when I had planned to grade a stack of papers and work on a new poem, I found myself babysitting an eight-year-old boy. Seated on my couch, he announced, "I can use my penis for a bookmark."

He was the only son of the woman who had suggested I come to Tuscaloosa. He was reading a children's book. I looked up from my computer, wincing slightly, trying not to give any indication I'd heard. I did not want to be doing this. I had not asked.

He would climb over me, setting his shoes in the recesses of my wheelchair, reaching around my shoulders, lifting himself up into my lap. The scabby knobs of his knees dug into my legs. I would try to talk him down.

It began with Clifford the Big Red Dog.

Needing papers signed, I went to Dana's office where she was grading. Her son was seated on the floor, watching a faded videotape. I made the mistake of identifying the dog, engaging the boy, and identifying myself as someone familiar with children. She looked up.

"Would you mind sitting with Calvin for a while?" she asked, tired. "I need to make some copies downstairs and I just can't take him."

Dana was up, already leaving. In reply, all I made was a noise.

Calvin came over, poking me with a finger, wordless.

"Let's not do that," I said. "Let's not poke each other."

He climbed up my leg and into my lap, where he watched

Clifford for an hour. When his mother returned, she scooped him up, distracted. I left, annoyed. No signature.

After that afternoon, every other week or so, Dana would find me wherever I was. In my office. In the mailroom. Going home. I was too young, too inexperienced to say no. I'd ruefully agree to look after the boy, drop whatever I was doing, offer up my wheelchair and body as a platform for his climbing.

The night he claimed his penis would fit into the pages of his book left me livid, disturbed. I wanted no more of what amounted to harassment, despite the mother's saccharine disingenuousness: *Calvin just loves you. And I know you love him.*

I resolved to say no the next time, to be free of it.

Spring had arrived early and the sky was a faded denim vault. Done for the day, I felt good. I whistled.

A block from home, at the edge of campus, where the road ran downhill to a freshwater spring, I crossed with the light. Then a car horn bleated.

I turned around. A car I didn't recognize had stopped in the road. Bright sunlight painted its windshield a solid coat of sun. I squinted, trying to see who the driver was. I moved closer to the curb, peering.

Before my eyes had adjusted, Dana was pulling Calvin from the car, dragging him by his twig of an arm to the sidewalk. I hadn't even recognized her, or her menace of a son, before she was climbing back into her car, calling over her shoulder she was late for a meeting and would be back in an hour.

And then Dana was gone. The boy and I looked each other over. Across the street was a Starbucks, first in the state of Alabama, it crowed. Sighing, I led Calvin in and bought him chocolate milk.

For a while, I thought we were the only ones there. An Eric Clapton album played throughout the store. I hated the boy a little more every moment.

Then a ragged woman sidled over, her jeans patched and patched and patched again. She sat down with something rolled up under her meaty arm.

It was a leather chessboard. As she unrolled it, she began to describe the foundation she had created for teaching underprivileged children how to play. Calvin, half feral, looked like he was ready to pounce on her.

Each time she shifted her plump frame in the seat, she groaned. She looked to me knowingly, as if pain were our bond, and by it we already knew one another.

Her teeth were horrors, used-up stumps, stained, broken.

"I've got lupus," she blurted. "Doctors are no good. But I don't have to tell you that."

I mumbled something noncommittal.

Calvin was a chess prodigy. He luxuriated in each match

with the woman, who seemed impressed at first, then indifferent and sour.

The day was gone and outside everything was dark. Through the long wall of glass, I could see cars disappearing around the curve, I could see the square of my apartment's one window, a low bronze light that was my desk lamp. When the Starbucks employees began to push vacuums around and look at us, his mother ran up, arms splayed out. I left, saying nothing. If I stayed, I might say some dire thing to any of them, to all of them, something black and regrettable.

The poems I wrote were sad, quieter than any I'd written before. Gone was any nod to slapstick. Monsters shrugged through them. Love was an unspoken ruin.

But they came quickly. Each day, I waited on one. At my keyboard, I read the news and dashed fragmentary e-mails to scattered friends.

I wrote about the invisible man. About Godzilla and Alice the Goon.

One night, having left her lab long enough to eat something, Ivy glanced at the computer screen, at first intrigued by the lines I'd written.

As she read further, her face soured.

"Why don't you just write about suicide, if that's what you want to do?"

"What do you mean?" I asked, angry.

She had thrown herself on my bed, staring up at the dropped ceiling, the fluorescent lights humming.

"Nothing," she said. "I don't mean anything. I just wish you would write something happy. For once. Something I'd like."

We barely understood one another. We hardly spoke the same language, it seemed sometimes. I turned back to the screen, to the poem, and closed it.

Eliot and I had become good friends. The sort to spot loose change on the ground, to pluck coins from a pay phone, Eliot had scavenger's eyes and the quick hands of a thief. He carried with him keys he found on campus, lost by custodians.

We were assembling manuscripts from new poems and old alike. I was obsessive: I printed new copies after the slightest changes, carrying them everywhere. When Eliot found a lab that printed out the university's paychecks and was otherwise dormant the entire month, when he discovered they'd print our manuscripts on the huge printers in seconds, we were regulars. An old man would hand them to us, wrapped in clear plastic, and warm, like white loaves of bread.

When Eliot no longer taught at the university, his non-tenure, nonrenewable contract expired, he found a lock mated to a key he had carried for years. Ten feet high and solid wood, on the third floor of a building that been an army barracks during the Civil War, rebuilt from rubble after Sherman burned the campus, the door pulled open, protesting.

Inside, a cavernous suite filled with junk, broken things, old printers, the slough and detritus of a university. It had started as storage space, progressed to trash heap, and was then forgotten.

Eliot whistled. I thought there was no way the space was usable.

A week's clearing out freed the space from the years. Ordered from a local print shop, a plate with his name and title and a made-up room number claimed it for his own. A call to the campus technology office finished the job.

Before the day was done, the place was furnished with a new computer, wired for Internet access. No one asked whether he taught there.

We spread our poems out on long tables, shuffling their order, adding new ones, pulling older ones from the mix. Eliot kept an electric putting green in the corner, practicing when stuck, unsure. Cheap wine chilled in a braying refrigerator. There were old couches. Vintage lamps lighting it all up. Sometimes at dusk we'd assemble balsa wood gliders and wind the rubber-band-powered propellers, launching them from the balcony, rooting for their rickety flight across the green grass below. Bats and moth wings swooped through the air.

From there we sent out into the world what we hoped were books.

When the call came, an instant nausea roiled inside me: the editor of New Issues Press, an imprint of Western Michigan University Press, wanted to publish my manuscript. A few months had passed since the day Eliot had walked with me to the campus post office, fat envelopes containing our manuscripts in his arms. Listening to the editor's gruff voice, I felt lightheaded, shocked even: assembling the manuscript, sending it out, and waiting by the mailbox every day for word, good or bad, to return had been processes separate from the writing of the poems, and though I'd hoped for this for years, I'd never allowed myself to think it might happen. Now that it had, I struggled to believe I wasn't dreaming. A year from then my book would come to be, an amazement. We hung up, and when I left my apartment, the February air was warm, and in it I laughed and laughed.

That October I woke up on a Wednesday morning in the emergency room with no idea why I was there. I remembered going to bed and seeing Ivy step into the bathroom. And then nothing, like tidal sleep had washed over me.

I'd had a grand mal seizure, my body shaking violently. When I was twenty-two, I'd suffered the first, reading poems at my desk. In intermittent years, a few seizures had followed. No neurologist could say much for certain, except that they weren't epileptic in nature and weren't the result of a tumor or other ailment. One suggested that maybe, when I broke my neck, I had suffered undiagnosed head trauma as well. Brain damage. All that was left to do was take medication and hope no more came.

By the time I was discharged, the sun was boiling up at the horizon's pink rim. Instead of going to bed, I ate a waffle at a diner near campus and left for my first class. I taught twice that day, as I did on Thursday and Friday as well. In the mailroom, friends and colleagues scolded me for even coming in. I finished the week, then left for my parents' home, where I stayed a week, resting, seeing my doctors. Eliot covered my classes while I was gone.

When I returned, Dana summoned me to her office. Her son was nowhere.

"We understand that you were away last week." She spoke in the plural.

At first, I was too fixated on this to reply. "Seeing my doctors," I finally said. "My neurologist."

"And who covered your classes?"

"Eliot covered them," I said. "Is there a problem?"

Dana looked out her window for a moment before turning back to me.

"We may not allow you to return to the classroom." She smiled blandly. "We may not even ask you to return next semester. To be determined."

I was stunned. I didn't say anything.

"And we understand you want to put yourself on the job market," Dana continued.

This was the crux of things, I thought, that I hadn't sought her help. I had applied for a handful of teaching jobs. So had Eliot. So had everyone who was not a student there.

"That's true," I replied.

"There are those of us—" Dana paused, letting the air punctuate, "who are concerned about your fitness for academia."

I didn't say anything.

"It can be grueling," she imparted, crossing her arms, leaning back.

I stayed silent. Anger was not an emotion that came easily to me. Not after my injury. But sitting there, I felt it.

"Have you ever considered career alternatives?"

"Like what?" I spat back.

"Like being a tutor," she said with relish. "A substitute teacher."

She leaned a little forward, to see the barb's sting. I sat back, mute.

"Is there anything you'd like to say?" she asked, a little crestfallen, robbed of something irreplaceably sweet.

"I think it's best that I say nothing."

An end comes in stages, an accumulation of failures or misfirings or injuries of every sort. Leaving that meeting, spattered by insult, any question in my mind was gone: I was leaving, whether I had a job or not. I stopped by Eliot's home, not far from my apartment. We sat at the base of his steps, plotting our exits.

He was optimistic, cheerful for my part, but looking down the car-lined street toward campus, I knew the remaining months would pass by quickly. And that would be the end of this. Not our friendship, but the romance of writing against something, the romance of contest, of opposition. We'd find new hindrances, I knew, but there had been something blessed and golden and hidden in that crummy town.

Soon, I would leave the town, and my friends, with no clear path ahead. The future like a pinhole seemed to wind in on itself, with little passage left for anything. Each day, on the way home, I practiced the hard words left between me and Ivy, who had fallen even more deeply into her work. Weeks and months had passed without the spark of affection we once had shared. All that was left was her exhaustion and my sense of failure. Though I had written the poems that soon would be my first book, I was leaving another town, with love like a vexing riddle in my mind.

When I found her waiting for me in the lamplight, I sighed, stopping in the open doorway. It was time to end things, to begin saying good-bye.

"Don't you want—" she said. "Do you want— We could go get an ice cream. Down the street. That place just opened."

"You have to give that test," I said, knowing she had to proctor an examination. "There's no way. No time."

"I could call someone," she said, unsure, I think, she meant it. "Get them to do it for me. We could go out one last time."

There it was. The words fell into the solution of the air.

"No, it's better this way."

She kissed my forehead, a trembling kiss, a collapsing kiss. And left. When the door clicked shut, I rested my head beside my keyboard. For a long time, I didn't move.

A freshwater spring came up from the ground near the road I followed to Eliot's duplex. The water made a reedy pond. We stopped by it one afternoon a few days before I was going to move. On a lark, we had purchased koi, brilliantly colored carp, from a local pet shop, and carried them flashing in plastic bags to the pond's muddy edge to release in the clear, cold water. We joked about returning after a long time to find the pond still teeming with life we had introduced to it, like an offering, a gift to commemorate our time in Tuscaloosa. We had three koi, orange and black and gold, metallic scales glinting in early spring sunlight.

Eliot slit the first bag open and poured it out: no longer than an index finger, the fish poured out like molten life and swam in long loops from the thickest reeds. I laughed and Eliot knelt down, taking off his glasses.

Then a wave shot from the pond's deep, dark middle.

The koi vanished with an audible pop. A sound like the water had been slapped with an oar. We watched stupidly, waiting for the koi to reappear.

For a long time neither of us spoke. Eliot still held two other bags in which koi, fish which can outlive humans, thrashed.

"Jesus," I said, a long, whistling sound.

When the water was still, and the ripples no longer ran to the grass, we looked at one another. Maybe whatever had devoured the fish was sated now. Maybe the other koi could be loosed into the water and live. Maybe we kidded ourselves, the owners of fish we had no place for. No place but this.

The second koi spilled from the bag like a doubloon. It fluttered forward and, again, we began to trust in our stupid hopes.

An identical wave rolled from the center of the pond. It came toward us. I cringed, and the same pop leaped up from the water like hunger itself. Gone.

"Fuck me," Eliot gasped. "Fuck me."

Eliot clambered down into the spring's mouth, a shallow hole where the water pooled, where he let the last koi go. For a few days, when he salted the water with fish flakes, it ate at the surface, motion and light and chance.

And then it was gone, too.

chapter

SIXTEEN

High above Baltimore, which was cloaked with dense snow, we circled a long, unnerving time: my mother had accompanied me just in time for the city to be crushed by a record, freak blizzard. It was my first flight, occasioned by the Association of Writers & Writing Programs conference, and the first time I'd see my first book. Even in that pregnant pattern through the storm-thick night, I loved being aloft, even when the jet shuddered in the unstable air and others gasped, clawed fiercely at armrests, arms, anything that held some hint of purchase. My mother hated flying. The whole flight, from Birmingham to Baltimore, she had studied fabric in her lap, sewing fitfully, and now leaned back against the seat, her eyes drawn shut. It was comical in its way, but I said nothing, all too aware of her sacrifice, her fear of the terrible height, all because I needed her help for the weekend I'd be there. I'd see my book and read from it, moments I'd long dreamed of, but these were dreams, somehow, that had, by their very nature, seemed likely to recede into impossibility. And yet, hours and altitudes away, I'd do both. We didn't discuss it, trading instead on the long familiar turns of family gossip. At last we began to nose blindly down towards Baltimore and all its wet snow and serrated wind.

"It's not that I'm afraid of dying," she said as the plane began to perceptibly pitch downward. Her eyes were shut, still, tighter now, her arms crossed, hugged close.

"No?"

"I know where I'm going when I die. I'm not worried about that."

By this she meant Heaven.

"Of course. Then what are you afraid of?"

"I'm not saying I'm afraid."

"I could be wrong, but I think that's exactly what you're saying."

The plane buffeted through bad air. Behind us, nervous gasps went up. My mother remained rock-steady, eyes shut tight.

"It's the falling. The descent. Knowing what's about to happen. That's what I don't like thinking about."

"Then don't think about it," I said, dryly.

This brought one of her eyes open for a baleful moment. She said nothing, went back to her imposed blindness. I chuckled aloud. We were close now, below the clouds, city lights winking in the night.

When the airline employee brought my chair up from the plane's cargo, where it had been disassembled, shoved in with all the suitcases, its frame was bent. The seat was at an odd angle and the electronic controls were in pieces in the seat. In that condition, there was no way to operate it. I was stunned: had they run over it? We insisted they fix it. The employees looked at me blankly, hoping I'd back down, go away. They radioed, then instructed us to have a seat, to wait. Two hours passed. A jet mechanic appeared, carrying an enormous wrench. He said nothing but bent the frame crudely back to a suggestion of its original shape. It was good enough.

An accessible cab, with a ramp that folded out for me to enter, rolled us slowly through the snowy streets. The hotel was dead, only employees standing around as though they remembered something regretful, all of them, all at once. In the lobby, the warmth of the heating was either oppressive or ineffectual when the lobby doors slid open and winter hissed in. Outside, a doorman stood in the cold. I walked out into the air to see the night and the snow which came down from the clouds like lace confetti. There was no noise. A softened hush. A mute hour.

We regarded each other with nods but didn't speak. I went inside.

The following morning I was scheduled to read from my book, even though I hadn't seen a single copy of it yet. When we awoke, a washed-out snowy light entered the windows. My mother pulled jeans up my legs, over my knees, helped me to turn side to side. She helped me sit, then stand and manage to gently fall back into my chair. My left arm was the first she threaded through a sleeve: because I'm unable to use it at all, the arm is tight, its tendons contracted, painful if stretched. After that, she washed my hair in the hotel sink, which was not particularly accessible, as most hotel bathrooms are not, even when claimed to be. A cheap vanity beneath the sink prevented me from coming close; I had to lean to the side. Water ran down my neck and into my lap. It was the best we could do.

All this was done without much comment. Cheap complimentary coffee spattered in the hallway, filling the hotel room with a burned tang. Despite the difficult sink, the routine had run like that for fifteen years' worth of mornings, except for when I had been away at school. What was there to say or acknowledge? Just the descent of snow from the sky, its dirty accretion, the wind stirring up white cork-screws before scattering.

Our hotel was far from where the conference was being held, and I was relegated to walking, or to exact change and the bus. I wanted to make my own way, to practice a kind of pained meditation on the hammering cold. But that was a kind of hypothermic roulette, I had to admit. I wanted to go early, see people I knew; my mother would attend the reading later. I knew I couldn't ask her not to be there, was not even sure I wanted that, but I felt a deep ambivalence: I couldn't hide my work any longer. It was time that it came into whatever its meaning would be in the world, and this included my family finally reading something I had written. I had no time to think much more about it. Downstairs and out I went, still plotting to walk the way.

Outside, my lungs recoiled from the freezing air. My legs began to ache. All the bones felt large with pain. I hurried to the corner, to the bus stop kiosk which stilled the air, but nothing warmed. I waited.

When the bus shambled into sight a long way up the empty street, I moved out of the kiosk, right up to the curb. I wanted the driver to see me, to know I was there, and if he swooshed by without stopping, as drivers often had when pressed for time, when the delay of fastening a wheelchair in place was too much to bear, I wanted to know, for my own self, I'd been seen, that the driver had made a choice.

The bus bore up to the curb and halted. The doors slid open and some warm air fell out like it had mass. The driver leaned over.

"This lift ain't worked in months," he said.

"What?"

"I done put the work order in more than once. But they never fix nothing."

"What am I supposed to do?" I asked, annoyed.

"You could wait for the next bus. Ten minutes. Maybe that lift will work."

He shrugged, spread his arms wide, as if he wanted to say it wasn't his fault. What could he do? The doors sealed back together like strange lips. The bus slid down the street, out of my sight. I retreated to the kiosk.

When the next bus came, the story was the same. I wanted to eye the driver, hard, wanted to say I knew better. But I was freezing. The air bit down on the lobes of my ears and my hands throbbed. I started away, toward the harbor, head down, eyes down, attempting to pretend I wasn't cold.

I thought I knew how to get there. I thought the way was straight. The sidewalk glinted with ice and my wheelchair swam across it, never quite stopping. I struggled to keep from sliding off the curb, spilling me into the street.

But the hotel never appeared, and no one I stopped seemed to know if it even existed. They looked at me like a riddle.

I was lost. There was no denying it, even if I hadn't strayed far. Waiting for a light to change and a crossing signal to flare, a man walked out of a building beside me. His manner was brisk as an arrow: he wasn't one to lose his way, whoever he was. And then I saw it: the shield on his heavy coat. A mailman. I asked him and his finger jabbed to the right. A few blocks, he said. The light changed and he bolted away, packages under his arm.

Behind me, the bright yellow building he had left sang its three notes: XXX. Electrified canary was the only color in that weather. Two stories up it went, immense, bold black text on its walls. Every taste, every desire, served inside.

I felt no warmer. I followed the postman's directions, toward the frozen creakings of the harbor. Before long, I saw the hotel, saw the scarfed throngs going in and out, their breath communal smoke.

I hurried in, all ache, and didn't stop inside the lobby until the cold couldn't reach. There, beside an ATM, I waited to thaw. Everything around me sang with bustle, but all I wanted was warm stillness. Time enough to feel my ears.

I looked down at my lap, nagged by something I couldn't quite identify. A dark, wet blot spread from my crotch outward. The bag I wore had malfunctioned, as it sometimes would. I groaned softly.

Because of my injury, my bladder operates purely on reflex, stimuli arcing from nerves to the spinal cord and back.

Maybe an hour remained until my reading. I wanted back the use of my arms and hands, more intensely than I had in a long time, if only to put them to violent misuse, to break something, to smash it fine, to make powder out of a whole thing.

Hoping to find a phone, and someone to help me use it, I scanned the lobby. The concierge tapped furiously at a keyboard. People milled around with lanyards bearing their names looped around their necks. There was no one I felt I could ask. No one whose eyes seemed open, uncommonly kind. I spend much of my time trying to read the content of people, their capacity for kindness. It was all too much, then. I feared I'd be forced to do my reading in that condition. To go before a crowd of strangers and say nothing of the obvious. To enter into a pained pact: *I will say nothing if you say nothing.*

And then I saw my mother, entering the hotel. I hurried over through the crowd.

"Good news," I said. I nodded downward towards the spreading wetness; she hesitated for a moment, considering.

"There's no way we can make it back to the hotel."

"Not in time, no."

"OK, wait here. I passed a Gap store on the way. I can run in, buy new jeans."

"And then what?" My mood was sour.

"What do you mean, then what?"

"Where do we change? How?"

"We'll figure something out. I'll be back."

She returned with a Gap bag. All we could think to do was enter one of the lobby restrooms, take it over, try to ensure no one entered. I backed my wheelchair against the door, hoping to block it, to effectively lock it shut. The challenge then was to remove the soaked jeans while I sat and then pull up the new pair, which would be even more difficult. I had some good strength in my legs; I could hold my body up a bit from the cushion I sat on. My mother tugged the wet denim down and tossed it into the sink; she'd rinse it when we were done. It was not easy and we had no time to struggle. She washed me with hand towels and runny soft soap. I knew the whole day I'd faintly smell of that gummy soap and urine, a mix that reminded me of disabled strangers I sometimes met who were poor or who received poor care. In malls, on streets, we would chat a bit, for what we shared. But, always, I thought, *We are not the same. I am not you.* I clung to that a long time, with shame.

People tried to enter the bathroom, slamming up against the door, shoving, apparently certain a little more force would let them in. We said nothing, trying to hurry, to waste no time with them.

The new jeans went on easier than I feared. I looked a

little rumpled, a little tossed about, but there was no help-
ing it.

We hardly said anything more, besides my quick thanks;
she was rinsing the old jeans in the sink, cupping handfuls
of soap into the filling basin. Her hair was a little astray.
She held the door open for me.

"I'll do something with these and then I'll be there. I
love you."

Looking back through the closing door, I saw her pause
for a moment, as though she took measure of the mirror.
And not her tired face. She took to cleaning the jeans as the
door swung to. Something inside me lurched.

The ballroom was already clotted with people when I entered; I paused in the doorway. I was nervous: a tingling in
my gut, an itch I could not find. I made my way to the table,
where the other poets waited: a group of us were to read. I
felt some small gratitude for that.

At the table, a copy of my book waited beside a glass
of water and a lapel microphone. On the cover, my name
seemed strange, like it wasn't mine in that first, dislocated
moment. The cover art suggested blood, an abstraction of
it, and I stared for a brief moment at it. I felt known, in a
way I hadn't expected, felt understood beyond what I even
understood of my work.

I'm not sure when I first imagined that I might someday

write a book, that it could be published, but somewhere in that blur of time and aspiration, I grew to hope on that book. And there it was, a physical thing, an object with mass, that took up some of the world's space. It seemed only barely real.

And then it was time to begin. In the audience, a few rows back from the front, I saw that my mother had slipped in. I smiled and nodded. Then it was my turn.

Whatever I read, whatever I said, I have no memory of it. Looking out, the audience seemed to swell like surf. I wasn't nervous, really, but it was more than I could digest. I read for my few short, shared minutes, hardly looking up from the page until the last line ran out of my mouth. There was applause, which I could hardly meet with my eyes. My mother hugged me, then retreated into the crowd. When I'd signed a few books, holding a pen in my mouth, and chatted with strangers, I left with my book beneath my left arm. The snow still sifted from the sky as I made my way back, flakes of it melting in my eyelashes, but I was warm.

The moment, all its sweetness, its potent surreality, began to recede when the jet lifted away from Baltimore. We sat in the same seats of the same jet. Aloft in frozen air, returning to another world, an old world. I looked out the window, high as I had ever been, and wondered what might now change.

EPILOGUE

Beside me, a man in a wheelchair quacks at a young woman pedaling past on a ten-speed bicycle. She seems weary, glaring over, and is gone. But, still, he's amused, self-satisfied, maybe a little daft. Solidly middle-aged, gray hair tied back into a ponytail, a bag of groceries precariously stowed on his lap, he never gives his name. I don't ask for it. Don't offer mine. We're waiting for a bus on a street corner in Atlanta. We've exhausted wheelchair talk: his is broken down, leaving him to push himself along slanted sidewalks and up steep hills. Mine? I've had it almost a year. Yeah, I like it well enough. There is a certain wild avidity in his eyes as he looks it over. I feel a little sad.

But then there is the quacking. And the awareness he is chatting up my fiancée. She trades banter with him pleasantly, though sometimes our eyes surreptitiously meet, acknowledging the weirdness of the moment. I stop talking. In the distance, a bus shambles into view. At last. We've been waiting almost an hour.

I'm not surprised when the bus driver leans out, his face marked with naked disgust. He's perturbed. We're slowing him down.

"I only have one spot for a wheelchair," he says, wishing he were anywhere but here. This said, he waits for us to sort it out, draw straws, guess a number.

"What do you mean?" I ask. But I already know.

"I mean the other spot don't work. The seats won't raise up out of the way. Y'all have to figure that out for yourself."

The quacking man gives up his spot almost immediately. But I tell him to wait, don't surrender so quickly. They have an obligation to be certain their equipment works properly, I tell him. Let them figure it out.

The driver reaches into his pocket, eyeing us, fishing out a cell phone. He turns his back, muttering unhappily, kneeling down, fiddling with a lever that won't move. He looks back at us over his shoulder. I smile back at him. I'm being wished out of existence. Out of his, at least. I've felt it before.

Soon, though, he's wrenched the seat up, folded it away. We all file on board the bus, and after he's belted our chairs down, he stomps on the accelerator.

Behind me, my fiancée falls quiet in the din and clatter, but the other man, still at my side, gabs on. I don't know him, won't ever see him again, but he doesn't feel like a stranger. I see him often, his type, his lonely, addled type, and have, for more than twenty years, feared that I could somehow become him someday.

I live in Atlanta now, with my fiancée. The long trek through small-town America that comprised most of my life is over, and there is a wonder at everything a large city provides: public transportation is a marvel, a novelty for me. Attempting to board a train downtown, two throngs converge at the car's whooshing doors: those exiting, those entering. I want on the train, but no one moves. A man sees me, begins to hector everyone around me.

"Wheelchair coming through," he announces, politely enough.

His tone is sensible but insistent. He's ignored. I smile at him, trying to wave him off, wanting no part of it. But he has a mission now.

"Excuse me, wheelchair coming through?" he announces a bit louder. "Come on, y'all! Man. In. A. Wheelchair."

Still, the cross currents of people pay him no mind. He decides to shout.

"*Respect!*"

Everyone jumps, snapped out of their private thoughts, then steps aside.

In the nursing home in the town I grew up in, where my grandfather is a surly patient, rendered mostly mute by a massive stroke and legless by amputations at his hips, the hallways stink of urine and nothing can change it. I hate to visit him there. This selfishness I confess: when I do go in to see him, I pray to see him sleeping in his bed. Or in no mood for company. The weight of the place is something I can't bear. Not even in my love for him.

A woman approached me in the hall once, while I waited to see him. Her hair was the color of dark ink, bottle false. She put her hand to my shoulder, leaning in, her wrinkled face a quilt of blotchy makeup.

"Finally," she cooed. "A good-looking resident around here."

A nurse pulled her away then. I tried a faltering smile. My face felt like paper devoured by flame. I left without seeing my grandfather. *Another time, another time*, I thought. But not then.

I escaped into the movie theater next door. I didn't care what was playing. Inside, the air was too cold, but I stayed.

■

That word scalded me. *Resident.* It was the password to every fear that had been inculcated in me since almost the first day of my paralysis. As much as the injury itself, undue hope can be debilitating: doctors, nurses, therapists work against its onset. I was told I'd never walk again, never feel anything. I would lead a benighted, circumscribed life. That was my challenge: to accept that granite fact.

I was twelve, a boy. Nothing more. Partly this was a gift. A mercy, even amidst the cruelty of stupid luck. Much of it saddened me, but that life, that life in which I was not even a full participant yet, it waited for me. And so it was easy to think of other things, to become an unexpected, unforeseen revision.

Years later, all those fears would return, having never really left, dormant seeds in the body's memory.

I knew that I would never find love. That no one could ever love me. Whatever I became in life, I was already stamped, fixed. The plasticity of youth gradually became the strictures of adulthood: in the most fundamental ways, I was no different from anyone. And, yet, I was set apart and always would be, and there were days and weeks and maybe even years when I thought there was no way that gap could be bridged.

Except perhaps with words. With writing. I think, looking back, I took to it with a desperation I never really apprehended. But with time that desperation didn't so much grow as it became uncovered, a dark ore to mine.

Someone speaks to me in the grocery store. A voice I don't quite recognize. I look up and it's a new neighbor, an architect who designs shopping malls. He's come here, he says, on his new electric bicycle: a false hip prevents any real exercise. I'm interested, ask questions about its operation: of all the work of the body, all its dalliances and meanderings, most recede from memory. How it felt to shave the green skin of an apple away from itself is foreign now. The dry cool of a stone is, I think, an abstraction, not so much remembered as supposed. But I can still feel in my legs the rhythms of pedaling, the work of balance against the earth, the rise of blisters from abraded flesh. All that is not so distant. It's yesterday.

I'm not certain he knows that as we talk, and a rude stream of consumers pass by, I'm far away, before the onset of these concerns, these fears.

And now I think that maybe I am beyond them.

We meet in another city. There for a writers' conference, I trudge back from dinner with friends through heavy rain.

The sidewalks fill up with it. The streets are foam white. Inside the hotel lobby, I say good-bye to my friends. Damp and tired, I want an end to the long day. No more talk. No more words.

Near the elevators, near the bar, I waver: though I want to go to sleep, I decide to look inside, passing through clusters of loud people, laughing, drinking, smiling. I hope to run into a friend. If not, I'll go to my room, where my mother and her friend Carolyn wait, having traveled with me.

I see two friends seated with others in a long booth against a window, and make my way through the crowd to them. For a few minutes I joke with one of them, glad I'm there no matter my fatigue. Rest is a renewable resource, I tell myself, but the opportunity to be with people who know me often feels rare. *This is why I'm here*, I think.

Then the other friend I had spotted is standing beside me, and with him is a woman I don't know. Longtime friends from graduate school, they've been to a reading and dinner tonight. He introduces us and goes back to his seat, leaving us to talk, though it's difficult in so much noise. Or it would be, if everyone and everything, all noise, all motion, didn't grow faint. There is only her.

Slight, with dark hair, eyes which never seem to drift, she is a writer. Instantly, I am awake, entirely certain she'll discover I'm a fool.

We talk about writing, novelists, poets I should include in a class I'd like to teach someday, an idea which slides about in the back of my mind and never gains much purchase, but as she speaks, as I begin to memorize her chin, her nose and mouth and eyes, an inexplicable focus begins to resolve the blur my life has been for all these years.

Why can't you be in my life?

We say good-bye after talking a long while, and I rise in the elevator, tired and heavy and sad. Sad that we live long miles apart. Sad that the world won't shrink. Sad that after all these years I have no idea how to be anything or anyone else.

At my hotel door, I hear the television inside. David Letterman. Loud. My mother and her childhood friend, giggling. I rap the door with my mouth stick. No answer. Another time, harder. No response. I knock my head against the door. I'm in the hallway. All down its length, room service trays gleam on the floor. Everything is still. Our room is a handicapped-accessible unit, with a button beside the door which loudly buzzes and flashes the room's lights when activated. A modification for the hearing impaired or the blind. I'm tired, confused, stuck here, and no one is in sight.

I press the button. A surprisingly shrill tone buzzes through the door. Inside, I can hear my mother and Carolyn jump up, and the television cuts off.

"Oh, shit," my mother drawls as Carolyn begins to laugh.

"Is it a fire?" Carolyn asks. "Hell, Paula."

"All I have to say is," my mother announces, "I have my pajamas on and I am not going out."

I mash the button like a car horn before the moment of collision.

"It's. Me. Paul," I almost shout into the door. "Your. Son. Knocking. On. The. Door."

The lock begins to rattle and the door opens. Inside, both women in their pajamas are cackling, a latter-day slumber party.

When I am in bed, and the lights go off, I wait a long while before sleep.

All day long I think of her, unable to say why, or, more truthfully, unable to admit that I have been smitten—in its truest sense, meaning *smite*, meaning I have been struck. I feel the force of it: inexplicable, undeniable. I wander through the hotel speaking to others, but I am thinking of her, saying her name, imagining another life.

That night I see her from a distance. Before I'm aware of it, I'm hurtling down the hallway. Toward her, calling her name, not exactly embarrassed by my lack of reserve, until I'm there. *E-mail me, please*, I say.

Though I can't stay, late for a poetry reading, when we say good-bye, I feel a part of my past begin to fall away.

■

At night, the faint percussions of trains rock by in the dark. My body never seems to fully surrender to sleep: one ankle throbs intermittently or a knee twitches its need to be stretched. I wake to little pains. The murmurs of disuse. Nerves signaling out in the distant dreams I never quite remember. Beside me now, mussed by the turns of sleep, her left arm laid across my rising chest, my fiancée dreams. She wears a blue Obama for Change T-shirt. This seems right. Corny, perhaps, but correct in a way I can't quite articulate. In her sleep she turns, winding the covers around her small frame. Because I can't hold on to them, I wake to see that I'm uncovered, my feet cold, my chest cold, but I smile, pierced by joy. I press my body, as best as I can, against hers, and there is enough warmth for sleep.

I want to say that every poem I've ever written was elegy to this simple moment. A presupposed elegy. Lament for what would never come if only because it had not yet arrived. But it'd be untrue, a fiction with an indulgent streak, veering toward a lie.

Whatever has happened to me, however it has left me, with bones brittled by lack of weight bearing, scars stippling my skin here and there like pale furrows, a fading memory remains of that younger self.

His name is my own, and our eyes are the same indefinite blue. Beyond that, we would hardly recognize one another, I think. We diverged in violence, half dead in the fullness of a summer not unlike this one.

To return to that moment when everything broke apart, when I was lifted up from the ground like the child I was and then lowered back like fragility itself is strange. Every day I am touched by that day's permanency, its long, dark, deepening shadow. Every day, and yet I hardly ever think back to it. One year, not long ago, I forgot my injury's anniversary for a week. I had to laugh.

And that is the heart of it: I laughed. The date was no longer a red mark on a dread calendar. Now there were only days. Now there were only months and years in unknowable succession. Now there is only time.

Tonight the sky is littered with an iridescent confetti of fireworks. They flare and rumble, setting unseen dogs to howling, afraid for everything they know their lives are. The falling fire soon runs out, cinders seeding a burned-up world.

And yet we look up, my fiancée and I, half enthralled, half absorbed in the talk we make with a friend. I'm thinking of this book, wondering how to bring it to its close, if not an end. Then I'm thinking of her. Of us.

And that is it.

July 4, 2009
Atlanta, Georgia

ACKNOWLEDGMENTS

That this book ever became more than a file on a hard drive is still a great amazement to me. Without the guidance and support of so many people, I could not have written it.

To my agent, Betsy Lerner, who set this in motion with an unexpected e-mail, I can't express enough gratitude. Her confidence in this book never wavered, even if mine sometimes did.

To my editor, Lee Boudreaux, who sifted through each meandering draft, I am indebted. Her enthusiasm carried me through bouts of frustration and fear, and her editorial genius saved the book from my mistakes.

To Daniel Halpern, and everyone else at Ecco, my inadequate, abiding thanks.

To family and friends, I owe more than just these words.

I would like to especially thank my parents and my brothers, who have never failed in their support. Also, Eliot Wilson, Mark Womack, Sean Torbett, and Chris Kerley, whose friendship has been a great gift. Also, Rodney Jones, Allison Joseph, Jon Tribble, Lucia Perillo, Ed Brunner, who once were teachers but now are good friends. Thank you, Jonette Larrew, for all your help and friendship. To Adam Turner, my cousin, thank you.

To Uche Nwokocha, my great thanks for your strength and assistance.

To Blas Falconer, Suzanne Frischkorn, Sharon Hayashi, Michael Salman, Reinaldo Román, Alexa Harter, Darby Sanders, Nora Gomez, Libby Gaalaas, Erin Kaczkowski, thank you for your parts in this story.

And to June, without whom this book could not exist, my love.